THE ELECTRIC SLIDE PROTEST:

Creative Protests for Social Change

Carrie Love

Lipsey & Love Legacy Press, LLC

application or misapplication of this information.

CONTENTS

Title Page

Copyright

Dedication

Introduction   1

Chapter 1: The Art of Disruption: Unleashing Creative Protests   7

Chapter 2: Resistance With Rhythms   22

Chapter 3: Art That Engages   39

Chapter 4: The Power of Laughter   48

Chapter 5: Protests and Pixels: Digital Activism   58

Chapter 6: Guerilla Gardening and Creative Grassroots   69
Protests

Chapter 7: Flash Mobs for Change   75

Chapter 8: Creative Policy-Driven Protests   82

Chapter 9: Conquering the Challenges & Criticisms   93

Chapter 10: Secrets of the Revolution: The Future of   100
Protests for the Next Generation

Conclusion: The Transformative Power of Creative   110
Activism

Curated Reading List for the Electric Slide Protest   115

Additional Recommendations: 119

References   120

Gratitude   125

About The Author   127

INTRODUCTION

Our lives begin to end the day we become silent about things that matter.
–Martin Luther King Jr., Civil Rights Leader

The Power of Traditional Protests:

Lessons From History

Protests have long been a vital tool for social change, serving as a voice for the voiceless and a platform for the marginalized. The 20th century offers numerous examples of traditional protests that shaped the course of history. The Civil Rights Movement in the United States, led by figures like Martin Luther King Jr., demonstrated the power of organized, nonviolent protest. Through marches, sit-ins, and boycotts, African Americans challenged systemic racism and demanded equality. A collective moral force that resonated across the nation propelled these actions, grounded in a deep understanding of injustice.

Similarly, Mahatma Gandhi's nonviolent resistance against British colonial rule in India is another cornerstone in the history of protest. Gandhi's concept of *satyagraha*, or truth force, emphasized nonviolent resistance as a powerful means of confronting oppression. Through mass civil disobedience, including the famous Salt March, Gandhi mobilized millions, inspiring movements for civil rights and freedom across the world. These traditional protests relied heavily on large gatherings, public demonstrations, and a clear moral message to bring about change.

However, the methods employed by the Civil Rights Movement and Gandhi's nonviolent resistance were not just about the physical acts of marching or sitting in. The Civil Rights Movement and Gandhi's nonviolent resistance employed carefully orchestrated performances to captivate the media and the public, transforming the struggles of the oppressed into an irresistible narrative. These movements were, in their own way, creative protests that used the tools available to them at the time to effect change. They laid the groundwork for the protests of today, but the world has changed, and so must our methods.

The Need for Innovation in Contemporary Protests

In the modern era, the landscape of activism has evolved dramatically. While the core principles of pursuing justice and equality remain unchanged, the means to achieve these goals must adapt to a rapidly shifting cultural and technological environment. Contemporary concerns such as climate change, digital surveillance, and global inequality require more dynamic and compelling approaches to capture the attention of increasingly distracted audiences.

Social media platforms inundate today's society with a constant stream of news, entertainment, and advertisements. Traditional protests, regardless of their just cause, often go unnoticed in this cacophony. Modern activists face the challenge of not only making their voices heard but also standing out above the noise. This necessitates protests that are not only visible but also memorable —protests that can cut through the clutter and resonate on a deeper level with a diverse and global audience.

This is where the need for creativity in protest becomes crucial.

Creative protests offer a means of engaging the public in ways that traditional methods may not. They are empowered to surprise, provoke thought, and evoke emotion in ways that are often more effective than a simple march or rally. Creative protests can also be more accessible to a broader range of participants, offering alternative means of engagement that go beyond physical presence at a demonstration. In a world where the fight for attention is fierce, creativity is no longer a luxury but a necessity.

Creativity as a Catalyst for Inclusivity and Engagement

One of the most significant benefits of incorporating creativity into protest is the way it lowers barriers to entry, making advocacy more approachable and inclusive. Traditional protests often require a significant commitment of time and energy, which can be a barrier for those unable to participate due to work, family responsibilities, or physical limitations. Creative protests, on the other hand, can take many forms—from online campaigns and art installations to flash mobs and street performances—allowing people to participate in ways that suit their abilities and schedules.

Creativity also builds a feeling of belonging and a sense of community. When people engage in creative acts of protest, they are not just making a statement; they are contributing to a collective experience that is often enjoyable and empowering. This sense of shared purpose can be particularly important in sustaining long-term movements, where maintaining momentum and motivation can be challenging. By making activism fun and engaging, creative protests can help keep participants energized and committed over time.

Furthermore, creativity allows for a broader range of voices to be heard. Traditional protests can sometimes be dominated by those who are most vocal or have the most resources, but creative protests open the door for a wider variety of participants. Artists, musicians, writers, and performers can all bring their unique skills to the table, enriching the movement and ensuring that it resonates with a broader audience.

Case Studies: Artistic Protests Around the Globe

Around the world, there are numerous examples of how creative protests have effectively brought attention to social issues and inspired change. In Chile, during the student protests of 2011, students used flash mobs—including a mass performance of Michael Jackson's "Thriller" dance—to draw attention to the need for education reform. These performances not only garnered media attention but also created a sense of solidarity among participants.

In Hong Kong, the 2014 Umbrella Movement used umbrellas as a symbol of resistance against police brutality. Protesters transformed these everyday objects into powerful symbols of defiance, creating striking visual imagery that captured the world's attention. The use of umbrellas was not just practical; it was a deliberate artistic choice that helped frame the narrative of the protests in a way that was both relatable and poignant.

In the United States, the "Die-In" protests, where participants simulate being dead to draw attention to issues such as police violence or healthcare, have been a stark and effective means of protest. These silent, somber displays disrupt public spaces, forcing onlookers to confront the reality of the protested issues, making them an impactful form of creative dissent.

These examples illustrate the potential of creative protests to transcend cultural and geographic boundaries, uniting people in a common cause through the universal language of art and performance.

Practical Strategies for Incorporating Creativity Into Activism

For activists looking to incorporate creativity into their initiatives, there are numerous practical strategies to consider. One of the most accessible is the use of visual art. Creating posters, banners, and murals that convey a message in a visually striking way can be an effective means of spreading a movement's message. Art installations in public spaces can also serve as powerful symbols of resistance, drawing attention to issues in a way that is both thought-provoking and engaging.

Another approach is to use performance art, such as flash mobs, street theater, or choreographed dances like the Electric Slide. Public spaces can stage these performances to surprise and engage passersby, provoking them to consider the presented issues in a fresh and unexpected manner. Performance art is particularly effective in its ability to capture attention and create a memorable experience for both participants and observers.

Digital activism also offers a wealth of opportunities for creativity. Social media campaigns that incorporate humor, satire, or viral challenges can reach a wide audience and generate significant attention for a cause. Additionally, digital art, including memes, videos, and animations, can be powerful tools for conveying a message in a way that is easily shareable and accessible.

Finally, incorporating elements of culture and tradition into protests can also be a powerful way to connect with people on a deeper level. Music, dance, and rituals that have cultural significance can resonate strongly with participants and observers alike, grounding the protest in a sense of identity and shared heritage.

Conclusion

While traditional forms of protest will always have their place in the fight for social justice, the challenges of the modern world require a more creative approach. By embracing creativity, activists can lower barriers to participation, sustain engagement over time, and make their message heard in a crowded and noisy world. The examples and strategies outlined in this introduction demonstrate that with a little imagination, protest can be not only powerful but also joyful, engaging, and inclusive. As we move forward, let us remember that the fight for social change is not just about what we are fighting against but also about how we fight. Creativity is not just a tool for protest; it is a way of reflecting the peaceful, just, and inclusive world of our collective dreams.

As we dive into the rich tapestry of creative protests, it's important to first understand the foundational role of disruption in activism. This disruption is not about chaos but about creatively challenging the status quo to inspire change. In the next chapter, we explore the art of disruption and how innovative protest strategies have historically captured attention and driven social change.

CHAPTER 1: THE ART OF DISRUPTION: UNLEASHING CREATIVE PROTESTS

There is no power for change greater than a community discovering what it cares about.
–Margaret J. Wheatley, American Writer
and Management Consultant

Introduction: The Power of Creative Protest

Protests have always been a powerful means of challenging the status quo, but in today's world, where information is abundant, and attention spans are short, traditional methods of protest can struggle to break through the noise. Creative protests, however, offer a unique solution to this problem. By harnessing the power of art, performance, and innovation, creative protests can captivate, inspire, and drive social change in ways that conventional protests may not. This chapter explores the art of disruption, examining the historical use of innovative protest strategies, the psychological mechanisms behind their effectiveness, and the insights we can learn from both real and fictional examples.

Contextual Background

Throughout history, protest has been a vital tool for the oppressed to voice their grievances and demand change. From the Civil Rights Movement in the United States to Gandhi's nonviolent resistance in India, protests have played a crucial role in shaping the world we live in today. However, as society evolves, so too must the tactics we use to effect change. The digital age has brought with it new challenges, such as the rapid spread of misinformation and the constant barrage of content competing for our attention. In this context, traditional forms of protest—marches, sit-ins, and demonstrations—often struggle to make a lasting impact. This is where creative protests come in.

Creative protests are not just about making noise; they are about making a statement that resonates on a deeper level. By using art, humor, and unexpected tactics, creative protests can cut through the clutter and engage people in ways that conventional protests cannot. They question the conventional norms of protest conduct and participation, thereby enhancing the accessibility and inclusivity of activism. In doing so, they open up new possibilities for engagement and inspire people to think differently about the issues at hand.

Escaping the Noise

Digital and media noise inundate the world, making it challenging to capture people's attention. The sheer volume of information available means that we are constantly bombarded with content, much of which is designed to distract rather than inform. The latest viral video or trending hashtag can easily overshadow traditional protests despite their power. To stand out, activists need to find new ways to capture the public's imagination.

Creative protests achieve this by breaking away from the expected and introducing elements of surprise and intrigue. Whether it's a flash mob in a busy city square, a piece of provocative street art, or a satirical performance that turns a serious issue on its head, creative protests grab attention in a way that is both engaging and thought-provoking. They draw people in, inviting them to become part of the experience rather than just passive observers. This not only makes the protest more memorable but also increases its impact by spreading the message further.

The Psychology of Engagement

Understanding the psychology of engagement is critical to comprehending why creative protests are so effective. Protests fundamentally revolve around communication, conveying a narrative that demands attention. The most successful protests are those that connect with people on an emotional level, making the issues feel personal and urgent. This is where storytelling comes into play.

Storytelling and Emotional Connection

Storytelling has always been a powerful tool for social change. It allows people to see the world from another's perspective and to feel their pain, their hope, and their struggle. Storytelling can humanize complex political issues during protests, making them more relatable and easier to understand. For example, during the Civil Rights Movement, the "I Am a Man" banners carried by African American men in Memphis, Tennessee, during the 1968 sanitation workers' strike served as a powerful reminder of the humanity and dignity of the protesters. These banners told a story of oppression, resilience, and the fight for equality in a way that resonated deeply with the public.

Creative protests often incorporate storytelling in innovative ways. They use symbols, metaphors, and narratives to convey their message, creating a powerful emotional connection with their audience. This emotional resonance is key to sustaining engagement over time. When people feel emotionally invested in a cause, they are more likely to stay involved and take action.

Humor and Surprise

Humor is another psychological tool that creative protests frequently employ. Humor can be a powerful way to disarm opponents, diffuse tension, and engage a wider audience. Satirical protests, in particular, use humor to critique power structures and expose the absurdity of certain policies or practices. The Yes Men, a group of activist-pranksters, are known for their satirical interventions, where they impersonate corporate or government officials and make absurd announcements that highlight the flaws in their policies. The Yes Men not only draw attention to important issues but also make them more accessible to a broader audience by using humor.

Surprise is another element that can make creative protests more engaging. When something unexpected happens, it captures people's attention and makes them curious. The Clown Army, an anti-war protest group that dresses up as clowns and performs in military-style formations, uses surprise and absurdity to disrupt the seriousness of military parades and other public events. By juxtaposing the playful and the serious, the Clown Army creates a powerful visual statement that challenges the status quo and invites people to question the meaning and purpose of military power.

Emotional Resonance and Lasting Impact

Finally, the emotional impact of a protest is what makes it memorable and effective in the long term. Creative protests that evoke strong emotions—whether it's anger, sadness, hope, or joy—are more likely to leave a lasting impression on those who witness them. For example, the "A Day Without Immigrants" strikes, where immigrants across the United States stayed home from work and school to demonstrate their importance to the economy and society, were not only impactful in their message but also deeply emotional in their execution. These strikes underscored the human cost of immigration policies and provided a voice to those frequently marginalized.

The "Black Lives Matter" street murals, painted in cities across the United States, serve as a powerful example of how art can effectively convey a message of justice and solidarity. These murals, often created by local artists and community members, serve as both a tribute to the victims of police violence and a call to action for systemic change. They are a visual representation of the movement's values and goals, and their emotional resonance helps to sustain the movement's momentum over time.

Key Takeaways

The key takeaway from understanding the psychology of engagement is that creative protests are effective because they tap into deep-seated emotional and psychological responses. By using storytelling, humor, surprise, and emotional resonance, these protests engage people on a level that goes beyond rational argument, making them more likely to remember the message and act on it. For activists, understanding these psychological principles can help them design more effective and impactful protests that drive social change.

Case Studies of Creative Protest

To further illustrate the power and potential of creative protest, it's helpful to look at specific examples from history, as well as fictional representations that offer valuable insights and inspiration.

Historical Examples

The Salt March (1930)

One of the most famous examples of creative protest is Mahatma Gandhi's Salt March in 1930. The British colonial government had imposed a tax on salt, making it illegal for Indians to collect or sell salt themselves. Gandhi saw this as an opportunity to challenge British authority in a way that was both symbolic and practical. Gandhi not only defied British law by leading a 240-mile march to the Arabian Sea to make salt from seawater, but he also galvanized a nationwide movement for Indian independence. The Salt March was a masterful example of creative protest, using a simple, everyday substance—salt—as a symbol of resistance and national pride.

The Umbrella Movement (2014)

In Hong Kong, the 2014 Umbrella Movement used umbrellas as a symbol of resistance against police violence and the erosion of democratic freedoms. Protesters used umbrellas to shield themselves from the police's use of tear gas and pepper spray, which inspired the movement's name. These umbrellas became a powerful symbol of defiance and solidarity, representing the protesters' determination to stand up for their rights despite the oppressive tactics used against them. The Umbrella Movement's use of a simple, everyday object as a symbol of resistance helped to capture the world's attention and highlight the protesters' cause.

The AIDS Memorial Quilt (1987-Present)

The AIDS Memorial Quilt is another powerful example of creative protest. The NAMES Project Foundation initiated the quilt in 1987 to honor the lives of those who had succumbed to AIDS. The quilt dedicates each panel to an individual who succumbed to the disease, serving as a memorial and a protest against the stigma and neglect experienced by those living with HIV/AIDS. Numerous locations around the world have displayed the quilt, raising awareness about the impact of AIDS and mobilizing support for individuals affected by the disease. The AIDS Memorial Quilt poignantly demonstrates the use of art as a tool for activism, transforming grief and loss into a powerful statement of solidarity and resistance.

Aboriginal Art Activism (1979)

In 1979, Aboriginal activists took a bold stand by walking out of the Hogarth art gallery with six paintings by Yirawala, a renowned Gunwinggu artist. This act not only aimed to reclaim artworks whose ownership had never received official recognition but also served as a powerful protest against the widespread exploitation of Indigenous artists. By removing these paintings, the activists brought global attention to the ongoing injustices faced by Indigenous communities in the art world, highlighting the need for greater respect and recognition of their cultural and artistic contributions.

Jesus and the "Extra Mile"

One of the earliest and most ingenious examples of creative protest comes from the teachings of Jesus Christ. Jesus instructs his followers, "If anyone forces you to go one mile, go with them two miles" (Holy Bible, N, NIV® 1984/2011, Matthew 5:41). Under Roman rule, soldiers could compel local residents to carry their gear for one mile, a burdensome and humiliating task. By suggesting that his followers voluntarily carry the burden for two miles, Jesus cleverly subverted the power dynamic. This act of passive protest placed the Roman soldier in an uncomfortable position, as they could not legally compel someone to carry their load beyond the first mile. This tactic of nonviolent resistance not only exposed the absurdity of Roman law but also empowered the oppressed by giving them a way to assert control over the situation without direct confrontation. Jesus' guidance to "exceed expectations" serves as a potent illustration of how innovative, nonviolent protest can upend oppressive structures and empower the marginalized.

Fictional Inspirations

Fictional representations of protest can also provide valuable insights into the power of creative activism. While these examples may not be real, they reflect the potential for creative protests to capture the imagination and inspire real-world action.

"V for Vendetta" (2005)

The film "V for Vendetta," based on the graphic novel by Alan Moore and David Lloyd, is a striking portrayal of the power of creative protest. The story follows V, a masked vigilante who uses theatrical acts of rebellion to challenge a totalitarian regime. V's use of symbols, such as the Guy Fawkes mask and the slogan "Remember, remember the fifth of November," along with his elaborate, performative acts of resistance, serve as powerful tools for mobilizing the public against oppression. The film demonstrates the transformative potential of art and performance in the struggle for freedom, highlighting how creative protest can inspire fear in those in power and hope in those oppressed.

"The Hunger Games" (2012–2015)

Another fictional example is the "Hunger Games" series by Suzanne Collins. The protagonist, Katniss Everdeen, becomes a symbol of rebellion against the oppressive government of Panem through her use of symbolic acts, such as the three-finger salute and the Mockingjay pin. These symbols, combined with her defiance in the face of overwhelming odds, ignite a nationwide uprising. The series illustrates how creative protest can be used to galvanize a movement, using symbols and narratives to unite people and inspire action. The fictional world of Panem serves as a powerful reminder of how creative resistance can challenge even the most entrenched systems of power.

The Transformative Power of Creative Protests

Creative protests have the power to transform not only the movements they are part of but also the societies they seek to change. By breaking away from conventional methods and embracing innovation, these protests can reach new audiences, sustain momentum over time, and inspire people to take action in ways they may not have considered before.

Reflecting on the Transformative Power of Artistic Protest

Protest art is a powerful call for social change. Its value as a tool in our arsenal should not be ignored. It speaks to our emotions, challenges our perceptions, and encourages us to see the world in new ways. Creative protests harness this power by turning activism into an art form, using creativity to make political statements that are both impactful and enduring. Whether it's a piece of street art that challenges the status quo, a satirical performance that exposes the absurdity of a policy, or a symbolic act of defiance that captures the imagination, creative protests have the ability to transform the way we think about and engage with social issues.

Encouragement to Think Outside the Box in Advocacy

The lesson for activists is clear: to be effective, we must be willing to think creatively. Traditional methods of protest still have their place, but in a world that is constantly changing, we need to be open to new ideas and new approaches. By embracing creativity, we can find new ways to engage people, sustain our movements, and ultimately drive social change. Whether it's through art, performance, humor, or storytelling, creative protests offer a powerful means of making our voices heard.

A Call to Action: Use Creativity as a Tool for Social Change

As we move forward in our fight for justice, let us remember that creativity is not just a tool for protest; it is a way of reimagining the peaceful, just, and inclusive world of our collective dreams. By using our creativity, we can find new ways to challenge oppression, engage our communities, and inspire change. So let us embrace the art of disruption and use it to build a better, more just world.

Key Takeaway

The key takeaway from this chapter is that creative protests have the power to drive social change by engaging people on a deeper level, sustaining momentum over time, and challenging the status quo in innovative ways. By understanding the psychology of engagement and drawing inspiration from both historical and fictional examples, activists can harness the power of creativity to make their voices heard and inspire others to join the fight for justice.

Derrick Bell's Fictional Electric Slide Protest

(1996): A Case Study in Creative Resistance

In the realm of creative protest, one of the most compelling examples comes from the imaginative work of Derrick Bell, an influential scholar and writer. Best known for his contributions to critical race theory, Bell also explored the concept of protest through fiction. One of his most intriguing and thought-provoking fictional creations is the "Electric Slide Protest," a narrative that serves as a powerful commentary on social justice, resistance, and the transformative power of collective action, particularly as expressed by African American women.

The Narrative of the Electric Slide Protest

African American women lead the Electric Slide Protest in Bell's fictional story, uniting to perform the popular line dance, the Electric Slide, at various public locations. These women, who face systemic oppression and societal marginalization, use the dance as an outward expression of the internal struggles they endure daily. The Electric Slide becomes a vehicle for them to resist the pressures of a society that often stifles their voices and disregards their experiences.

The dance itself is both simple and symbolic. As the women move in unison, their synchronized steps represent unity and solidarity against the forces of racism, sexism, and social injustice. The Electric Slide Protest takes place in public spaces where these women would otherwise feel invisible or oppressed, transforming these environments into stages for their resistance. By engaging in this joyful and rhythmic protest, the women reclaim their power, making a bold statement that is both a celebration of their identity and a challenge to the status quo.

The Symbolism and Impact of the Electric Slide Protest

Bell's fictional protest is rich with symbolism, reflecting the resilience and creativity of African American women in the face of adversity. The choice of the Electric Slide—a group dance associated with celebration, community, and cultural pride—highlights the importance of joy and unity as forms of resistance. For these women, the dance is more than just a performance; it is a way to assert their presence, demand recognition, and resist the societal forces that seek to marginalize them.

The Electric Slide Protest serves as a reminder that effective resistance can take many forms and that creativity can be a powerful tool in the fight against oppression. By choosing to dance in public spaces, these women challenge societal norms and expectations, turning acts of marginalization into moments of empowerment. The dance invites spectators to join in, breaking down barriers between the protesters and the public, and transforming passive observers into active participants in the movement.

Lessons from Bell's Fictional Protest

Derrick Bell's fictional account of the Electric Slide Protest offers several important lessons for contemporary activists, especially those working within marginalized communities:

1. **The Power of Subversion**: The Electric Slide Protest exemplifies how creative actions can subvert expectations and disrupt the status quo in ways that traditional protests may not. By disguising their

protest as a harmless dance, the participants are able to engage in resistance without immediately triggering defensive responses from those in power.

2. **Joy as Resistance**: Bell's narrative underscores the significance of joy and positivity in activism. For these African American women, dancing becomes a radical act of self-expression and resistance. It shows that protest can celebrate life, culture, and resilience without being confrontational or somber. This approach helps sustain movements over time, keeping participants motivated and engaged.

3. **Inclusivity and Accessibility**: The simplicity of the Electric Slide dance makes it accessible to a wide range of people, regardless of age or physical ability. This inclusivity is a crucial element of the protest, as it allows more people to participate and feel a sense of ownership and belonging within the movement.

4. **Cultural Resonance**: By choosing a dance that is deeply embedded in African American culture, the Electric Slide Protest taps into shared experiences and collective memory. This cultural resonance amplifies the impact of the protest, helping to spread its message more effectively and creating a strong sense of community among participants and observers alike.

Connecting Fiction to Reality

While the Electric Slide Protest is a fictional creation, its themes and strategies are highly relevant to real-world activism, particularly within marginalized communities. Throughout history, various forms have successfully employed the strategy of using art, culture, and creativity to challenge power structures.

Derrick Bell's story reminds us that the most effective protests confront injustice and empower, opening up new ways of interacting with the world and each other.

Derrick Bell's Electric Slide Protest encapsulates the central message of this book: that creative, joyful, and inclusive actions have the power to disrupt entrenched systems of power and inspire lasting social change. By drawing on the lessons from this fictional protest, activists today can explore new and innovative ways to make their voices heard and to build movements that are not only effective but also deeply resonant and sustaining.

Conclusion

Derrick Bell's vision of the Electric Slide Protest goes beyond mere storytelling, serving as a model for leveraging creative resistance to effectively and empowering confront injustice. By weaving together elements of art, culture, and collective action, Bell's fictional protest offers a vision of activism that is as imaginative as it is impactful. As we continue to explore the art of disruption in this chapter, the Electric Slide Protest stands as a testament to the transformative potential of creative protest, reminding us that the fight for justice can be both serious and joyful, both challenging and celebratory. For the African American women in Bell's story, the Electric Slide becomes a dance of defiance, a powerful symbol of their resistance and resilience, and a call to all of us to find creative ways to push back against oppression and injustice.

While disruption paves the way for activism, emotional resonance often amplifies the power of protest. Few things connect and mobilize people more effectively than music and dance. In the following chapter, we explore how rhythms of resistance have unified movements and convey powerful messages through the universal language of music and dance.

Toolkit

Checklist for Planning a Disruptive Protest:

- Define your objective: What change are you trying to bring about?

- Identify your target: Who or what is your protest aimed at?

- Plan the disruption: Choose a method that is creative, nonviolent, and impactful.

- Gather resources: What materials, people, and permissions (if any) do you need?

- Prepare for consequences: Consider legal, social, and political repercussions.

Actionable Steps:

- Start small with a local issue that needs attention.

- Use visual or performance art to capture attention in public spaces.

- Collaborate with local artists, musicians, or performers to enhance the protest's impact.

CHAPTER 2: RESISTANCE WITH RHYTHMS

If I can't dance to it, it's not my revolution. –Emma Goldman, Anarchist and Political Activist

Introduction: The Power of Music and Dance in Protest

Music and dance have always been integral to the human experience, transcending cultural and linguistic barriers to convey deep emotional truths. In the realm of protest, these forms of expression hold a unique power: they can unify diverse groups, sustain morale, and amplify the message of resistance in ways that words alone often cannot. This chapter delves into the historical use of music and dance in protest movements and their continued potency as powerful tools for social change today. By examining the universal language of music and the metaphorical power of movement, we will uncover how these creative forms of resistance can inspire and mobilize communities, turning collective action into a powerful force for change.

The Impact of Music and Movement in Protest

Crossing Cultural Barriers

Music and Dance as Universal Languages:
One of the most significant strengths of music and dance in protest is their ability to overcome cross-cultural and linguistic barriers. People from diverse backgrounds can understand and feel music and dance on an emotional level, unlike spoken language. This makes them particularly effective in protests that seek to unite individuals across different cultures and communities.

Examples of Global Protest Movements:
Songs like "Bella Ciao," an Italian folk song that became the anthem of the anti-fascist resistance during World War II, have transcended their origins to resonate with protestors across the globe. "Bella Ciao," originally a song about the partisans who fought against Mussolini's fascist regime and Nazi occupation, encapsulates the spirit of resistance and the fight for freedom. Its lyrics, which speak of sacrifice for a greater cause, have made it a powerful symbol for movements far beyond Italy. From student protests in Europe to demonstrations against authoritarianism in Latin America, "Bella Ciao" has been adopted by diverse groups as a universal cry for justice and liberation. It is simple yet stirring melody and message of standing against oppression continue to inspire new generations, proving that music can be a potent force in rallying people together for a common cause.

Protest movements around the world have repurposed and embraced cultural expressions like the Haka, a traditional dance of the Maori people of New Zealand. Originally performed by Maori warriors to display strength and unity, the Haka has evolved into a powerful expression of defiance and solidarity. In recent years, the Haka has been used in various contexts, from climate change protests to movements against social and racial injustice. The intense physicality, rhythmic chanting, and fierce expressions of the Haka convey a deep sense of communal power and resistance, making it an effective tool for unifying protestors and asserting a collective identity. By adapting the Haka for modern protests, activists honor its cultural roots while also transforming it into a global symbol of unity and resistance.

These examples demonstrate how cultural expressions, whether through music or dance, can transcend their original contexts and become potent symbols in global movements for justice and change. These cultural forms' adaptability allows for their reinterpretation and repurposing, providing a voice to the struggles of diverse communities worldwide. At a time when social movements are becoming more interconnected across borders, songs like "Bella Ciao" and the Haka, with their universal messages, serve as powerful tools for expressing solidarity, resistance, and hope.

Creating Powerful Collective Experiences

Music and Dance Fostering Solidarity

Music and Dance as Catalysts for Unity:
When individuals come together to sing or dance in protest, they create a powerful sense of solidarity. The act of moving together in rhythm or harmonizing in song builds a collective identity, reinforcing the shared purpose of the protestors. This collective experience can be empowering, providing protestors with the strength to continue their fight.

Historical and Contemporary Examples:
The use of "We Shall Overcome" during the Civil Rights Movement in the United States is a powerful example of how a song can unify and sustain a movement. Civil rights activists adopted "We

Shall Overcome," originating from gospel and folk traditions, as a hymn of perseverance and hope. Its simple, repetitive lyrics and melody allowed protestors from all walks of life to join in, regardless of their musical ability, creating a shared experience that transcended individual differences. Sung in churches, during marches, and at sit-ins, the song served as a source of emotional strength and a rallying cry for those confronting brutal opposition. The act of singing together in the face of adversity helped to reinforce the protestors' commitment to nonviolent resistance and their belief in the eventual triumph of justice. The song's message of enduring faith and solidarity resonated deeply within the movement, binding people together in their struggle for civil rights and equality.

In modern times, the concept of collective action through song and performance has evolved with the rise of flash mobs—spontaneous gatherings where participants suddenly perform a choreographed routine in a public space, often to the surprise of onlookers. These flash mobs have been effectively utilized in various forms of activism, from environmental campaigns to political protests. The pre-choreographed dances, set to music that often carries a symbolic message, are powerful tools for capturing attention and conveying a movement's message in a way that is both visually and emotionally impactful. Environmental activism, for instance, has used flash mobs to highlight the urgency of climate change, with participants performing dances that symbolize the planet's fragility or the destructive impact of human activity. Similarly, political protests around the world have employed flash mobs to convey messages of solidarity and resistance, using the element of surprise and the power of collective movement to draw attention to their cause.

These modern forms of protest draw on the same principles that made "We Shall Overcome" so powerful: the ability of music and collective performance to unite people, create a sense of shared purpose, and convey a message that resonates on both an emotional and intellectual level. Whether through the enduring refrain of a song or the sudden eruption of a choreographed dance, these expressions of unity and defiance continue to play a crucial role in mobilizing support and drawing attention to social and political causes. Like "We Shall Overcome" did during the Civil Rights Movement, they show how the arts can amplify the voices of those seeking change, creating moments of solidarity that can transcend cultural and geographical boundaries.

Decoding the Universal Language of Music

Evoking Deep Emotional Connections

Music as an Emotional Amplifier:
Music has the unique ability to evoke deep emotional responses, making it a powerful tool in protest. Whether it's the stirring lyrics of a protest song or the haunting melody of a hymn, music can amplify the emotional impact of a protest, helping to convey the gravity of the issues at hand.

Examples of Emotional Connections in Protest Music:
Bob Dylan's 1962 song, *Blowin' in the Wind*, became a rallying song for both the civil rights movement and the anti-war movements of the 1960s, capturing the complex emotions and aspirations of a generation yearning for change. The gentle song asks, "How many roads must a man walk down before you call him a man?"—directly questioning civil rights, justice, and peace. Dylan's lyrics, deceptively simple yet deeply evocative, spoke to the universal longing for justice and the frustration with the slow pace of societal progress. The refrain, "The answer, my friend, is blowin' in the wind," suggested that the solutions to these pressing issues were elusive yet omnipresent, waiting to be recognized and acted upon. This ambiguity resonated with listeners who were grappling with the moral and ethical dilemmas of their time, making the song a unifying force in the movements it supported.

The song's folk melody and Dylan's plaintive delivery added to its power, making "Blowin' in the Wind" not just a piece of music but a vehicle for collective reflection and action. It became a soundtrack for marches, sit-ins, and protests, its words echoing the hopes and frustrations of those fighting for civil rights and peace.

Similar to this, the 1976 release of "Zombie" by Fela Kuti, which targeted the military dictatorship that ruled Nigeria with an iron fist, became a powerful tool of resistance. Fela Kuti, a pioneer of the Afrobeat genre, used music as a weapon to critique the oppressive regime, and "Zombie" was one of his most impactful works. The song's infectious rhythms, driven by Kuti's characteristic blend of jazz, funk, and African rhythms, drew listeners in, but it was the biting lyrics that delivered the sharpest blows. In "Zombie," Kuti likened Nigerian soldiers to mindless zombies who obeyed orders without thought or question, blindly enforcing the will of a corrupt and brutal government. The song's chorus, repeating the word "Zombie," became a stinging insult that resonated with the public, many of whom were already disillusioned with the military's role in their country.

"Zombie" did more than just entertain—it provoked. The song's boldness in criticizing the military regime made it a rallying cry for those who opposed the government's abuses of power. Fela Kuti's fearless expression of anger and frustration through his music inspired others to speak out, even at great personal risk. Despite the military's harsh response, which attacking Kuti's compound and brutalizing him and his family, the song's impact remained unabated. "Zombie" became a symbol of resistance, embodying the courage to confront tyranny and demand change. Like Dylan's "Blowin' in the Wind," Fela Kuti's "Zombie" used the power of music to articulate the sentiments of a movement, turning rhythm and rhyme into potent tools of social and political change.

Both songs, though from different cultures and addressing

different struggles, demonstrate the universal power of music to inspire, mobilize, and challenge the status quo. "Blowin' in the Wind" and "Zombie" became more than just popular songs —they were anthems that encapsulated the spirit of resistance, urging listeners to question, feel, and act. Their poignant lyrics and compelling melodies helped fuel movements that sought to dismantle oppression and build a more just and equitable world. In this way, both songs serve as enduring reminders of how art and activism can intersect, using the emotional power of music to drive social change.

Using Music as a Source of Motivation

Music as a Motivational Tool:
Protest music can serve as a source of motivation for activists, helping to sustain morale during long and arduous campaigns. The repetitive nature of many protest songs, combined with their often hopeful or defiant lyrics, can provide a sense of continuity and purpose, reminding participants why they are fighting and what they hope to achieve.

Examples of Motivating Protest Songs:
Public Enemy's "Fight the Power," released in 1989, emerged as one of the most potent anthems of resistance against racial injustice, particularly within the African American community. The song, with its unapologetically bold lyrics and aggressive, driving beat, served as both a rallying cry and a declaration of defiance against the systemic racism and oppression that had long plagued the United States. "Fight the Power" was written during a time when issues of racial inequality were once again coming to the forefront of national consciousness. It resonated deeply with those who were frustrated with the persistent disparities in justice, economic opportunity, and social treatment of Black Americans.

Chuck D's powerful delivery of lines like "Elvis was a hero

to most, but he never meant shit to me" challenged the mainstream narratives that had long marginalized Black culture and contributions. The song called out the hypocrisy and double standards of a society that celebrated certain figures while ignoring or undermining the contributions of Black people. Its chorus—"Fight the power!"—became a mantra for those who were fed up with the status quo and ready to push back against systemic oppression. The accompanying music video, directed by Spike Lee, further amplified the song's impact, showcasing scenes from a protest march in Brooklyn, with images of crowds raising their fists and demanding change. "Fight the Power" was not just a song; it was motivational music that inspired a new generation to engage in the struggle for civil rights and social justice.

Similarly, the protest anthem "Ain't Gonna Let Nobody Turn Me Around" played a crucial role in the Civil Rights Movement of the 1960s, becoming a staple at marches, sit-ins, and rallies across the South. African American spiritual tradition, a source of strength and solidarity in the face of adversity, rooted the song with its repetitive, call-and-response structure. As activists faced brutal opposition—from police violence to legal intimidation—the simple, resolute message of "Ain't Gonna Let Nobody Turn Me Around" reinforced their determination to continue the fight, no matter the obstacles.

The song's structure, which invited participation from everyone within earshot, helped to unify protestors, creating a powerful sense of collective identity and purpose. As voices joined together in the chorus, "Ain't gonna let nobody turn me around, turn me around, turn me around," the song became a powerful declaration of resilience and unwavering commitment to the cause of justice. Sung during some of the most pivotal moments of the Civil Rights Movement, such as the Selma to Montgomery marches, it provided emotional sustenance to those risking their lives for the right to vote and the broader cause of racial equality.

"Fight the Power" and "Ain't Gonna Let Nobody Turn Me Around" showcase the lasting influence of music in motivating, uniting, and empowering those involved in the fight for justice. While "Fight the Power" brought the energy and defiance of hip-hop to the fight against modern-day racial injustice, "Ain't Gonna Let Nobody Turn Me Around" drew on the rich tradition of spirituals and freedom songs that had long provided solace and strength to African Americans. Despite their differences in style and era, both songs served as rallying cries for their respective movements, helping to motivate activists and sustain them through the challenges they faced.

These anthems show how music can transcend mere entertainment to become a powerful tool for social change. Songs like "Fight the Power" and "Ain't Gonna Let Nobody Turn Me Around" not only reflect the spirit of resistance but also help to shape it, turning individual voices into a collective force capable of challenging and changing the world by expressing the emotions, frustrations, and hopes of a community.

Movement as Metaphor

Using Dance and Music as a Form of Expression

Dance as a Form of Protest:
Dance, akin to music, serves as a potent medium for conveying resistance and defiance. Through choreographed movements, dancers can embody the emotions and messages of a protest, using their bodies to convey what words cannot.

Examples of Dance in Protests:
Capoeira, a dynamic and multifaceted martial art that originated among African slaves in Brazil, stands as a powerful symbol of resistance and cultural preservation. Developed in the 16th century by African people who were brought to Brazil by the

Portuguese slave trade, Capoeira was much more than a mere fighting technique; it was a covert form of rebellion against the brutal conditions of slavery. The enslaved people ingeniously disguised their combat training as a form of dance, blending elements of music, acrobatics, and spirituality into the practice. This allowed them to prepare for potential uprisings and defend themselves from oppressive forces while maintaining a connection to their African heritage.

Capoeira's fluid, dance-like movements, and the rhythmic music played on traditional instruments like the berimbau created the illusion of a cultural ritual rather than a form of combat, allowing practitioners to train under the watchful eyes of their oppressors without arousing suspicion. Capoeira's art became a means of preserving cultural identity in the face of relentless efforts to erase it. It was also a form of psychological and physical resistance, offering a sense of empowerment and community among the enslaved. Over time, Capoeira evolved into a rich cultural expression that encapsulates the resilience, creativity, and spirit of resistance of its practitioners. Even after slavery was abolished, Capoeira continued to thrive, eventually becoming a symbol of Afro-Brazilian identity and pride, as well as a global phenomenon that resonates with people fighting against oppression and for cultural preservation.

Similarly, the Dabke, a traditional Arab folk dance, has taken on profound significance in the context of Palestinian resistance, serving as both an expression of cultural identity and a symbol of defiance. Traditionally performed at weddings and celebrations across the Levant, the Dabke features a line of dancers holding hands or shoulders, performing synchronized steps and stomps to the rhythm of traditional music. In Palestine, however, the dance has transcended its celebratory roots to become a powerful act of resistance against occupation and a reaffirmation of connection to the land.

In the face of ongoing displacement and attempts to erase

Palestinian culture, the Dabke has been used in protests and demonstrations as a way to assert cultural identity and unity. The dance's strong, rhythmic movements, which are often performed in public spaces, symbolize the steadfastness and resilience of the Palestinian people. By performing the Dabke in the streets, at protests, and in front of Israeli checkpoints, Palestinians reclaim their cultural heritage and assert their presence on the land that is central to their identity. The collective nature of the dance, with participants moving in unison, embodies the sense of community and solidarity that is crucial to the Palestinian resistance. In addition to strengthening the bonds among participants, the Dabke sends a powerful message of unity and resistance to the world, demonstrating how cultural traditions can serve as tools of protest and expressions of national pride.

Both Capoeira and the Dabke demonstrate the profound role that cultural expressions can play in movements for resistance and liberation. Rooted in specific historical and cultural contexts, these art forms have adapted to address the challenges of their times, transforming into powerful symbols of identity, resilience, and defiance. They show how music, dance, and martial arts can be more than just cultural practices; they can be acts of resistance that preserve the spirit of a people, empower communities, and challenge oppression. In this way, Capoeira and the Dabke continue to inspire and mobilize those who seek to assert their cultural identity and fight for their rights, standing as testaments to the enduring power of cultural resistance in the face of adversity.

Symbolic Gestures

Dance as a Symbolic Act:
Many protests use dance not only as a form of expression but also as a symbolic gesture that conveys a deeper message. The dance's movements, location, and performance all contribute to

its symbolic significance, transforming the act of dancing into a powerful statement of resistance.

Examples of Symbolic Dance:

The toyi-toyi, a vibrant and dynamic dance of protest, holds a significant place in the history of South Africa's anti-apartheid movement. In the 1980s, South African activists adopted the toyi-toyi, a powerful tool of resistance against the oppressive apartheid regime, from the military drills of Zimbabwean freedom fighters. The dance is characterized by its high-energy, rhythmic stomping and chanting, often performed in unison by large groups of protestors. The physicality of the toyi-toyi served multiple purposes: It was a form of exercise that kept protestors energized during long marches, a display of collective strength and unity that intimidated the apartheid forces, and a way to build morale among participants. The sheer force and synchronization of the movements symbolized the resolve and solidarity of those fighting for freedom and equality, turning the streets into stages of defiance and hope.

The toyi-toyi's impact extended beyond its physical performance. It became a symbol of the anti-apartheid struggle, embodying the spirit of resistance that fueled the movement. The chants that accompanied the dance often included slogans and calls for liberation, amplifying the voices of those who had been silenced for so long. The toyi-toyi was not just a dance; it was a declaration of resilience, a way for the oppressed to assert their presence and demand change. The sight and sound of thousands of protestors moving and chanting together sent a powerful message to the apartheid regime and the world: the people of South Africa would not be broken, and their fight for justice would not be denied.

Derrick Bell, a legal scholar and civil rights advocate, has reimagined the Electric Slide, an African-American group line dance popular at most family and community activities, as a metaphor for synchronized, joyful resistance. In Bell's interpretation, the dance represents more than just coordinated movement—it symbolizes the power of unity and collective action in the face of systemic oppression. The Electric Slide, with its simple steps and repetitive, flowing movements, becomes an accessible and inclusive form of expression that can bring people together in a shared experience of resistance and empowerment.

The Electric Slide demonstrates how dance, in the context of protest, not only unites participants but also infuses a sense of joy and celebration into movements that are often characterized by struggle and sacrifice. The synchronized dance reinforces the power and uplifting nature of resistance, transforming a mere choreographed routine into a profound statement of solidarity. Participants in the Electric Slide remember the strength that comes from working together toward a common goal by linking arms and moving as one. This sense of unity is essential in any protest movement, as it helps to sustain momentum and inspire hope even in the face of adversity.

Both the toyi-toyi and the Electric Slide demonstrate the transformative power of dance in protest movements. The toyi-toyi, with its vigorous, rhythmic movements, conveys strength, defiance, and a refusal to subdue, while the Electric Slide, with its joyful and inclusive nature, offers a more subtle yet equally potent form of resistance. Each dance, in its own way, highlights the importance of collective action and the ability of cultural expressions to galvanize people, build community, and inspire change.

These dances show that resistance is not solely about confrontation; it is also about the celebration of identity, the affirmation of solidarity, and the creation of spaces where people can come together to express their hopes, dreams, and demands for a better future. Whether through the defiant stomps of the toyi-toyi or the coordinated steps of the Electric Slide, dance becomes a language of protest that transcends words, conveying the emotions and aspirations of those who are fighting for justice. In this way, the toyi-toyi and the Electric Slide are more than just dances—they are enduring symbols of the power of movement, both literal and metaphorical, in the struggle for freedom and equality.

Past Reflections and Modern Impact

Historical Context of Music and Dance in Protest

Historical Examples of Music and Dance in Protest:
Throughout history, music and dance have played crucial roles in protest movements. Enslaved Africans in the United States used spirituals as a form of covert resistance, and the labor movement used anthems to express dissent, build solidarity, and inspire action.

Case Studies of Historical Impact:
The song "Strange Fruit," originally performed by Billie Holiday in 1939, stands as one of the most haunting and powerful protest songs in American history. Written by teacher and songwriter Abel Meeropol, the song poignantly addresses the brutal reality of lynching in the United States, particularly in the South. Through stark and vivid imagery, "Strange Fruit" depicts the bodies of Black men and women hanging from trees, likening them to the "strange fruit" that rots in the sun. The song's mournful melody and evocative lyrics convey a deep sense of sorrow and outrage, serving as a poignant condemnation of the racial violence that plagued the nation. By bringing the horrors of lynching into the public consciousness, "Strange Fruit" became not only a chilling testament to the suffering of Black Americans but also a powerful tool of protest that challenged listeners to confront the realities of racial injustice. Its impact resonated far beyond the jazz clubs where it was first performed, making "Strange Fruit" a timeless anthem of resistance and a chilling reminder of America's dark past.

Modern Applications of Music and Dance in Protests

Contemporary Examples:

In recent years, social media has amplified the reach and impact of protest music and dance, allowing these forms of expression to go viral and inspire movements across the globe. Flash mobs, for example, have become a popular form of protest, using the element of surprise and choreographed dance to draw attention to various causes, from climate change to political corruption.

The Role of Technology and Social Media:

Platforms like YouTube, TikTok, and Twitter have revolutionized the sharing and consumption of protest music and dance. Songs like "This Is America" by Childish Gambino and movements like the viral "Jerusalema" dance challenge have shown how music and dance can transcend borders and inspire global movements for change.

The Evolving Role of Music and Dance in Activism

The Ongoing Relevance of Music and Dance in Protest:

As new challenges and opportunities arise, the role of music and dance in protest continues to evolve. These forms of expression remain powerful tools for activists, offering a way to connect with audiences on an emotional level, build solidarity, and amplify the message of resistance.

Encouragement for Future Activists:

For future activists, the lessons of the past are clear: music and dance are not just supplementary to protest but are central to its power and impact. By harnessing these forms of expression, activists can create protests that are not only effective but also deeply resonant and inspiring.

Conclusion

The power of music and dance in protest lies in their ability to evoke deep emotional responses, create powerful collective experiences, and transcend cultural barriers. From historical examples like "We Shall Overcome" and the toyi-toyi to contemporary movements amplified by social media, these forms of expression have been integral to the success of protest movements around the world. As we look to the future, it is clear that music and dance will continue to play a vital role in creative activism, offering a universal language of resistance and hope that can inspire and mobilize people across the globe. We encourage activists to embrace these forms of expression, utilizing them to craft protests that are not only potent but also joyful and inclusive, bringing people together in the pursuit of justice and change.

Just as music and movement can galvanize people, visual art holds the power to encapsulate complex messages and spark deep reflection. Art is more than just an accessory to protest; it is a form of activism in its own right. In the next chapter, we delve into the world of protest art, exploring how visuals can engage, inspire, and drive movements for change.

Toolkit

Checklist for Organizing a Music or Dance Protest:

- Choose a theme: What message do you want to convey through music or dance?

- Select the format: Is it a flash mob, a concert, or a public performance?

- Arrange logistics: Secure a location, permissions, and sound equipment if necessary.

- Promote the event: Use social media, posters, and word of mouth to gather participants.

- Prepare participants: Provide choreography or song sheets in advance.

Actionable Steps:

- Use music and dance that are culturally relevant to your audience.

- Integrate call-and-response songs to engage the crowd.

- Video and share the event online to reach a larger audience.

CHAPTER 3: ART THAT ENGAGES

Art is not a mirror held up to reality, but a hammer with which to shape it. –Bertolt Brecht, German Playwright and Poet

Introduction: The Power of Art and Symbolism in Protest

Art has the unique ability to communicate what words cannot, transcending language, culture, and barriers to evoke emotions and inspire change. In protest movements, art and symbolism serve as powerful tools to express collective grievances, hopes, and dreams. They distill complex issues into compelling visual narratives that resonate deeply with people, uniting them around a shared cause and mobilizing them for action. This chapter delves into the role of visual art, symbolism, and digital platforms in modern protests, exploring how they transform individual complaints into a shared, powerful language of resistance.

The Canvas of Change: Visual Art in Activism

Visual art has long been a medium through which activists communicate messages of dissent and hope. By harnessing the power of imagery, artists can convey complex ideas and emotions in ways that words alone cannot. From street art and graffiti to poster art and graphic design, visual art has the power to inspire, challenge, and mobilize people for social change.

Graffiti and Street Art in the Hood

Art in Public Spaces:
Street art and graffiti are among the most direct forms of protest art, often appearing in public spaces where they can reach a broad audience. Activists use these art forms to circumvent traditional media channels, delivering their messages directly to the streets, where they command attention.

Examples of Impactful Street Art:
Street art has been a powerful tool in protests around the world. For example, the work of Banksy, an anonymous street artist, often critiques political and social issues through provocative and thought-provoking imagery. Murals depicting George Floyd's face and the words "I Can't Breathe" appeared on walls across the globe in response to the George Floyd protests, serving as both memorials and calls to action.

The Role of Graffiti in Gentrification Protests:
Marginalized communities have used graffiti as a form of protest against gentrification, reclaiming their neighborhoods and resisting displacement through art. In cities like New York and London, graffiti artists have painted powerful messages on walls to draw attention to the social and economic impacts of gentrification.

Poster Art and Graphics

The Tradition of Poster Art in Activism:
Social movements have long used poster art as a portable, reproducible form of protest that is easy to distribute and display.

Posters can simplify complex ideas into striking visuals that capture attention and convey powerful messages.

Examples of Influential Poster Art:
The iconic "Hope" poster of Barack Obama by Shepard Fairey became a symbol of the 2008 presidential campaign, representing a message of change and optimism. Similarly, posters from the Women's March on Washington in 2017 featured bold graphics and slogans that emphasized unity and resistance against oppression.

The Evolution of Graphic Design in Modern Protests:
With the advent of digital technology, graphic design has become even more versatile and accessible as a tool for protest. Digital posters and infographics can be shared widely on social media, reaching a global audience and amplifying the message of the movement.

Symbolism in Movements: Crafting Identity and Unity
In protest movements, symbols play a crucial role, transforming complex ideas into simple, recognizable emblems that a wide audience can easily understand and adopt. These symbols help to create a sense of identity and unity within the movement, serving as rallying points for collective action.

The Peace Sign

Origins and Design:
The peace sign, originally designed by British artist Gerald Holtom in 1958 for the Campaign for Nuclear Disarmament, has become one of the most widely recognized symbols of peace and protest worldwide. The designers combined within a circle the semaphore signals for the letters "N" and "D" to call for global nuclear disarmament.

Global Adoption and Impact:

Antiwar movements around the world, including the Civil Rights Movement in the United States, quickly adopted the peace sign. As a simple symbol of peace and non-violent resistance, it crosses language and cultural barriers.

Legacy and Continued Relevance:
Decades after its creation, the peace sign remains a potent symbol in protests against war, violence, and injustice. Its enduring relevance demonstrates the power of a well-crafted symbol to inspire and unite people across different contexts and generations.

The Rainbow Flag

Creation and Symbolism:
The rainbow flag was created by artist Gilbert Baker in 1978 as a symbol of LGBTQ+ pride and rights. Each color in the flag represents a different aspect of the LGBTQ+ community, with the rainbow as a whole symbolizing diversity and inclusion.

Visibility and Solidarity:
The rainbow flag has become an iconic symbol of the LGBTQ + rights movement, prominently displayed at pride marches and other events around the world. Its vibrant colors and simple design make it a powerful visual statement of visibility and solidarity, celebrating the diversity of the community and the ongoing fight for equality.

Global Impact and Adaptation:
The LGBTQ+ community has adapted the rainbow flag over the years, adding additional stripes to represent marginalized groups like people of color and transgender individuals. This evolution of the flag highlights its flexibility as a symbol that can grow and change with the movement it represents.

Artistic Acts: Performance Art and Symbolic Gestures

Performance art and symbolic gestures use the human body and movement to convey powerful messages and create compelling narratives within protest movements. These acts often involve the physical presence and participation of activists, transforming protest into a visceral and emotional experience.

"Die-Ins" and Silent Protests

The Power of Stillness and Silence:
"Die-ins" and silent protests are forms of performance art that use stillness and silence to draw attention to the consequences of violence, disease, or injustice. These protests often involve participants lying on the ground as if dead, symbolizing the lives lost or affected by the issue at hand.

Historical Examples of Die-Ins:
During the AIDS crisis in the 1980s and 1990s, the activist group ACT UP used die-ins to protest government inaction and raise awareness about the epidemic. These protests were powerful visual statements that forced the public to confront the human toll of the crisis.

The Effectiveness of Silent Protests:
Various movements have also used silent protests to emphasize the seriousness of the issues they are protesting. For example, in 1789, the Women's March on Versailles was a silent march of women demanding bread and political reform, using the absence of sound to emphasize the urgency of their demands.

The Black Lives Matter Plaza

Transforming Public Spaces:
Street renaming and public mural creation are powerful symbolic gestures that transform everyday spaces into sites of resistance and remembrance. One such example is the Black Lives Matter Plaza in Washington, DC, where a large mural reading "Black Lives Matter" renames and paints a section of the street.

Impact and Significance:
The Black Lives Matter Plaza has become a focal point for protests against racial injustice, serving as a physical space where people can gather to express their solidarity and demand change. The mural itself has become a symbol of the movement, representing the ongoing fight for racial equality and justice.

Global Examples of Similar Acts:
Other cities around the world have taken similar actions, such as the "End Racism Now" mural in Raleigh, North Carolina, and the painting of "Black Lives Matter" on streets in cities across the United States. These public art acts help to reclaim public spaces and assert the presence and importance of the movements they represent.

The Digital Gallery: Social Media as a Platform for Protest Art

In the digital age, social media platforms have become vital spaces for the creation, sharing, and amplification of protest art. These platforms allow artists and activists to reach a global audience, creating virtual galleries of resistance that transcend geographical boundaries.

Viral Art Campaigns

The Spread of Digital Protest Art:
Viral art campaigns use social media to quickly spread images, videos, and other forms of digital art that convey the message of the movement. These campaigns can rally support and raise awareness on a global scale, often using hashtags to connect related content.

Examples of Viral Campaigns:
The #BlackLivesMatter movement has seen the widespread sharing of digital art that amplifies its message, from illustrations and graphics to videos and memes. Similarly, the #MeToo movement has used visual art to spotlight stories of sexual harassment and abuse, rallying support for survivors and pushing for systemic change.

The Power of Hashtag Activism:
Hashtag activism has emerged as a potent tool for disseminating protest art online, enabling users to effortlessly locate and distribute content associated with a specific movement. This form of activism has the potential to create a global community of supporters united by a shared visual language of resistance.

Memes as Protest Art

The Intersection of Humor, Art, and Activism:
Memes are a form of digital art that condenses complex ideas into simple, often humorous images or videos that are easily shareable. In the context of protest, memes can be used to critique political leaders, policies, or societal norms in a way that is accessible and engaging.

Examples of Political Satire Memes:

People have used memes to ridicule political figures, like the "Not My President" memes that surfaced following the 2016 US presidential election. These memes use humor and satire to engage audiences, making political commentary more relatable and digestible.

Engaging Younger Audiences:
Memes are particularly effective at engaging younger audiences, who are often more attuned to the fast-paced and visual nature of social media. By using humor and brevity, memes can make complex political issues more approachable, encouraging participation and activism among digital natives.

Conclusion

Art and symbolism in protest movements go beyond mere decoration; they are powerful tools for communication, identity formation, and mobilization. Whether through the striking imagery of street art, the unifying power of symbols like the peace sign and the rainbow flag, or the visceral impact of performance art and digital campaigns, art has the ability to transform individual grievances into a shared language of resistance. In a world where visual communication is increasingly important, the role of art in activism will only continue to grow, offering new ways to inspire, engage, and effect change. We encourage activists to harness the power of art to craft compelling narratives that deeply resonate with people and propel the movement forward.

Artistic expression in protests often challenges authority and evokes strong emotions. But there is another, often underestimated, tool that can disarm opponents and draw attention: humor. Even the most serious issues can become approachable with humor and satire, and in the upcoming chapter, we will explore how protesters have used laughter as a potent weapon.

Toolkit

Checklist for Creating Effective Protest Art:

- Define the message: What issue are you addressing, and what do you want people to take away?

- Choose your medium: Paintings, murals, installations, posters, or digital art?

- Identify locations: Public spaces, social media, or art galleries?

- Consider impact: Will your art shock, inspire, educate, or provoke thought?

- Prepare materials: Gather supplies, collaborate with other artists, and plan the installation.

Actionable Steps:

- Organize a community art day where locals can contribute to a larger piece.

- Use stencils or wheat paste to quickly apply art to public spaces.

- Partner with local galleries or businesses to display protest art.

CHAPTER 4: THE POWER OF LAUGHTER

A satirist is a man profoundly revolted by the society in which he lives. His rage takes the form of wit, ridicule, mockery. –Gore Vidal

Introduction: The Role of Humor and Satire in Activism

Humor has long been a tool of resistance, a way to critique power structures, highlight injustices, and foster a sense of community among activists. Far from undermining the seriousness of a cause, humor personalizes and humanizes it, reminding us that even in the struggle for justice, there is room for joy, resilience, and hope. This chapter delves into the use of humor and satire in protest movements, both historically and in contemporary times, with the aim of disarming opponents, engaging the public, and promoting social change.

The Mechanisms of Humor and Satire in Activism

In activism, humor works on multiple levels. It can serve as a coping mechanism, a way to defuse tension, and a tool for critiquing authority. By using humor, activists can present their message in a way that is accessible and engaging, while also disarming their opponents and encouraging critical reflection among their audience.

- **Disarming Opponents:** Humor can soften the impact of criticism, making it more difficult for those in power to retaliate without appearing overly harsh or humorless. This can create a safer space for activists to express dissent and critique.

- **Engaging the Public:** Humor can make complex or controversial issues more relatable and easier to understand. It can also attract media attention, helping to amplify the message of the protest and reach a wider audience.

- **Fostering Solidarity:** Shared laughter can create a sense of community and solidarity among protestors, strengthening the bonds within a movement and boosting morale.

Historical Examples of Humor in Protest

Throughout history, humor has played a key role in protest movements. From medieval jesters who used satire to critique authority to modern activists who used humor to highlight social injustices, humor has proven to be a powerful tool for resistance.

The Jester Activists/Fools

- **Historical Role of Jesters:** In medieval courts, jesters held a unique position where they could speak truth to power under the guise of humor. Their ability to critique kings and nobles without fear of retaliation made them pioneers of sarcastic protest.

- **Jesters as Truth-Tellers:** Jesters were often seen as wise fools who used humor to reveal uncomfortable truths. Their role as truth-tellers disguised as humorists allowed them to challenge authority and societal norms in ways that others could not.

- **Modern Parallels:** Today, satirists and comedians like Jon Stewart, Stephen Colbert, and John Oliver continue this tradition by using humor to critique political leaders and policies, holding those in power accountable through wit and satire.

The Yes Men

- **The Yes Men's Activism:** The Yes Men are a duo of activists known for their elaborate pranks on corporations and political institutions. By impersonating officials and creating fake websites, they highlight the absurdity and injustice of certain policies and practices.

- **Notable Actions:** One of their most famous actions was creating a fictitious New York Times edition announcing the end of the Iraq War, which sparked widespread discussion about the media's role in perpetuating war.

- **Impact of Their Work:** The Yes Men's pranks often draw significant media attention, forcing the public to confront the issues at hand and sparking debate on critical topics. Their work demonstrates the effectiveness of using humor and satire to expose societal injustices and challenge the status quo.

Modern Movements and Digital Media's Role

In today's digital age, humor and satire have found new platforms on social media and online outlets, where memes, viral videos, and satirical news stories can quickly spread and reach global audiences.

Memes as Digital Protest Signs

- **The Rise of Memes in Activism:** Memes have become a popular form of digital protest, condensing complex issues into simple, shareable images that can quickly spread across social media platforms.

- **Cultural Relevance:** By including current cultural references, memes are entertaining and engaging, perfect for grabbing people's attention. By tapping into popular culture, activists can connect with a broader audience and make their message more accessible.

- **Examples of Memes in Protest:** During the 2020 U.S. presidential election, memes were widely used to critique candidates, policies, and societal issues, helping to shape public opinion and mobilize voters.

Satirical News and Commentary

- **The Role of Satirical News:** Platforms like "The Onion" and TV shows like "The Daily Show" use satire to provide a humorous take on current events, highlighting the absurdities and injustices in politics and society.

- **Public Impact:** Satirical news can influence public opinion by presenting serious issues in a humorous context, making them more approachable and encouraging critical thinking among audiences.

- **Educational Role:** Satire also serves an educational purpose, informing audiences about current events and societal concerns in an entertaining way that is often more engaging than traditional news sources.

Crafting Effective Humorous Protests

To create effective humorous protests, activists must strike the right balance between humor and message, ensuring that the comedy enhances the protest's impact rather than detracting from it.

Understanding Your Audience

- **Tailoring Humor to Your Audience:** Effective humor necessitates an understanding of the audience's cultural and contextual background. What may be funny to one group may be offensive or confusing to another.

- **Cultural Sensitivity:** Activists must consider cultural nuances and sensitivities when crafting humorous content to ensure that the message is received as intended and does not alienate potential supporters.

- **Focused Messaging:** Different audiences respond to different types of humor, so it is important to tailor the comedic approach to the specific context and goals of the protest.

Balancing Humor and Message

- **Preserving the Core Message:** While humor can be a powerful tool for highlighting important issues, it is essential to maintain the clarity of the protest's primary message. Humor should amplify the message, not overshadow it.

- **Examples of Effective Humor:** Satirical posters and slogans at protests, such as the "Keep Your Rosaries Off My Ovaries" sign used in reproductive rights marches, effectively use humor to convey a serious message while keeping the focus on the cause.

- **Strategic Use of Humor:** Activists should use humor strategically to emphasize key points, ensuring that the protest's underlying message remains clear and impactful.

The Power and Pitfalls of Using Humor in Activism

While humor can be a powerful tool for activism, it also comes with potential risks and challenges that activists must navigate carefully.

Misinterpretation

- **Risks of Miscommunication:** Misunderstandings of humor are common, particularly among diverse or global audiences. What is intended as satire may be taken literally, leading to confusion or backlash.

- **Examples of Misinterpretation:** There have been instances where satirical content was misinterpreted as genuine, leading to unintended consequences or undermining the protest's credibility.

- **Clear Messaging:** To reduce the risk of misinterpretation, activists must craft their humorous content with clarity and precision, ensuring that the intended message is evident to the audience.

Sensitivity to Context and Cause

- **Respectful Humor:** Humor in activism must be used with care to ensure that it does not trivialize the issues at hand or offend those it aims to support. Activists must strike a balance between being humorous and remaining respectful of the cause.

- **Balancing Act:** The challenge lies in creating humor that is both impactful and sensitive to the context. Successful examples, such as the satirical art of Banksy, often walk this fine line, critiquing societal issues while maintaining a level of respect for those affected.

- **Potential Pitfalls:** If not handled carefully, humor can backfire, alienating potential allies or diminishing the perceived seriousness of the cause. Activists must be mindful of these pitfalls and use humor strategically to enhance, rather than undermine, their message.

The Great Pothole Parade: A Fictional Example of Satirical Protest

In the bustling city of Bumpyville, the residents had long suffered from a plague of potholes that turned every commute into an off-road adventure. Despite numerous complaints and petitions, the city council remained as inert as the asphalt that refused to coalesce into smooth roads. In a stroke of satirical genius, the community decided it was time for action—but not the kind you'd expect.

Led by the self-appointed "Mayor of Potholes," a group of citizens organized "The Great Pothole Parade." On a sunny Saturday, the streets were abuzz with anticipation as spectators gathered to witness this unprecedented event. Instead of marching to demand road repairs, participants creatively decorated the potholes along Main Street, turning them into works of art and spectacle.

They transformed one pothole into a miniature swimming pool, complete with tiny diving boards and plastic swimmers basking in the murky water. Toy astronauts and space rovers transformed another pothole into a "moon crater," exploring its depths. Yet another was transformed into a "giant's cereal bowl," filled with colorful balls and a giant spoon.

As the parade commenced, the "Mayor of Potholes" led the procession, riding a car with specially adapted wheels to navigate the treacherous terrain. Behind him, a float carried a live band playing the theme song of the day: "Hole-y Moly, What a Town!" Participants followed, each stopping to present their creatively adorned pothole to the cheering crowd while volunteers handed out "I Survived Bumpyville" bumper stickers.

The parade not only brought laughter and camaraderie to the community but also caught the attention of the media. Local and national news outlets covered the spectacle, highlighting the residents' plight and their innovative form of protest. The images of the decorated potholes went viral on social media, sparking discussions about infrastructure and civic engagement across the country.

Mounting public pressure and the embarrassing spotlight finally spurred the city council into action. The city council dispatched repair crews within weeks, leading to improvements in Bumpyville's streets. People hailed the Great Pothole Parade as a triumph of creative protest, a testament to the power of satire to effect change.

In the aftermath, the residents of Bumpyville celebrated not only smoother commutes but also the strength of their community. The Great Pothole Parade became an annual event, commemorating the victory and reminding everyone of the impact of collective action—especially when seasoned with a dose of humor.

This fictional example demonstrates the engaging, creative, and effective use of satire in protest to draw public and media attention, thereby catalyzing change. By turning a common frustration into a public spectacle, the residents of Bumpyville were able to not only achieve their goal but also create a lasting legacy of community spirit and resilience.

Conclusion

Humor and satire are powerful tools in the activist's arsenal, capable of disarming opponents, engaging the public, and fostering a sense of solidarity within movements. By understanding the mechanisms of humor and carefully crafting their message, activists can use laughter to amplify their cause, challenge authority, and inspire change. However, with this power comes the responsibility to use humor wisely, ensuring that it supports the cause and resonates with the intended audience. As we continue to fight for justice, let us remember that laughter is not only a weapon of resistance but also a reminder of our shared humanity and the hope for a better world where joy and justice go hand in hand.

While humor can break down barriers, technology is breaking down borders. The digital age has transformed the way we communicate, organize, and protest. In the following chapter, we explore the rise of digital activism, where pixels and hashtags have become the new tools of revolution, connecting voices across the globe for collective action.

Toolkit

Checklist for Using Humor in Protests:

- Identify your target: What or who are you satirizing?
- Plan your message: What truth are you revealing through humor?
- Choose your medium: Street theater, memes, parody videos, or comedic performances?
- Test your content: Ensure your humor is appropriate and doesn't alienate potential allies.
- Prepare for backlash: Consider how your humor might be received by different audiences.

Actionable Steps:

- Create satirical posters or flyers that mock the opposition's stance.
- Organize a comedy night focused on social justice themes.
- Develop humorous social media content that can go viral.

CHAPTER 5: PROTESTS AND PIXELS: DIGITAL ACTIVISM

The power of social media is it forces necessary change. –Erik Qualman, American Author, and Digital Marketing Expert

Introduction: The Digital Era of Activism

The digital revolution has fundamentally transformed the landscape of protest and activism. By merging technology with creativity, digital activism has ushered in a new era where voices from across the globe can unite in the pursuit of justice and change. This chapter explores how digital platforms, tools, and strategies have empowered activists to mobilize, raise awareness, and effect change on an unprecedented scale. We will delve into the rise of digital activism, examine the tools used to mobilize the masses, explore the power of online petitions and crowdfunding, and discuss the challenges and risks associated with digital protest.

The Rise of Digital Activism

The advent of the internet and social media has democratized access to communication tools, enabling individuals and groups to share their messages with a global audience. Digital activism, also known as cyberactivism or e-activism, leverages these platforms to amplify voices, organize protests, and advocate for social and political change.

- **Democratization of Communication:** Digital platforms like Twitter, Facebook, and Instagram have provided a space for underrepresented voices to be heard. Unlike traditional media, which often requires significant resources and connections, digital media allows anyone with internet access to participate in activism.

- **Key Moments in Digital Activism:** Often cited as one of the first major movements driven by digital activism, the Arab Spring began in 2010. Social media platforms played a crucial role in organizing protests, sharing information, and rallying international support. Similarly, the #MeToo movement, which gained momentum in 2017, used digital platforms to highlight the prevalence of sexual harassment and assault, leading to widespread social and cultural change.

- **Impact of Digital Activism:** Digital activism has proven to be a powerful tool for change, enabling activists to bypass traditional gatekeepers, reach a global audience, and build momentum for their causes. From grassroots movements to global campaigns, the digital realm has become a critical space for activism in the 21st century.

Mobilizing the Masses

One of the most significant advantages of digital activism is its ability to mobilize large groups of people quickly and efficiently. Through encrypted communication, viral hashtags, and social media campaigns, activists can coordinate protests, share information, and build solidarity across borders.

Encrypted Communication

- **Security and Anonymity:** Encrypted communication apps like Signal and Telegram have become essential tools for activists. These platforms offer secure messaging services that protect the privacy of users, allowing them to communicate and coordinate without fear of surveillance or repression.

- **Encryption Mechanisms:** Using end-to-end encryption, these apps guarantee that only the intended recipients can access the messages. This security feature is crucial for activists operating in repressive environments where government surveillance is a significant threat.

- **Case Studies:** During the Hong Kong protests in 2019, activists used Telegram to organize flash mobs and share real-time updates on police movements. The app's encryption and anonymity features provided a safe space for protestors to coordinate their efforts without exposing themselves to government retaliation.

Viral Hashtags

- **Global Reach:** Hashtags have become powerful tools for spreading awareness and uniting people around common causes. Movements like #BlackLivesMatter and #FridaysForFuture have used hashtags to mobilize support globally, connecting activists and supporters across different countries and cultures.

- **#BlackLivesMatter:** This hashtag has played a pivotal role in the global fight against racial injustice. It began as a response to George Zimmerman's acquittal in the killing of Trayvon

Martin in 2013 and has since grown into a worldwide movement. The hashtag has brought together millions of people to demand justice and accountability for victims of police violence and systemic racism.

- **#FridaysForFuture:** Initiated by Greta Thunberg in 2018, this hashtag has galvanized young people around the world to demand action on climate change. The movement has organized global climate strikes, drawing attention to the urgent need for environmental sustainability and climate justice.

- **Impact of Viral Hashtags:** Hashtags are effective in raising awareness, rallying support, and creating a sense of community among activists. They enable movements to transcend geographical boundaries and build global networks of solidarity.

The Power of Online Petitions and Crowdfunding

In addition to mobilizing people, digital platforms also provide tools for activists to gather support and resources through online petitions and crowdfunding campaigns. These tools empower individuals to take action and contribute to causes they care about, amplifying the impact of their efforts.

Online Petitions

- **Platforms like Change.org and Avaaz:** Online petition platforms have become vital tools for activists seeking to influence policy changes and hold corporations accountable. These platforms allow users to create and sign petitions, which can then be delivered to decision-makers.

- **Successful Campaigns:** Online petitions have led

to significant changes, from policy reforms to corporate responsibility initiatives. For example, a petition on Change.org successfully pressured Starbucks to adopt a comprehensive recycling program, and another campaign on Avaaz contributed to the suspension of a major dam project in Brazil's Amazon rainforest.

- **Engagement Strategies:** Effective petitions often include compelling narratives, clear demands, and strong visuals that resonate with the target audience. By engaging supporters emotionally and intellectually, these petitions can gather the necessary momentum to bring about change.

Crowdfunding Campaigns

- **Platforms like GoFundMe and Kickstarter:** Crowdfunding platforms allow activists to raise funds for various aspects of their campaigns, from legal fees and logistics to creating protest art and media content. These platforms enable individuals and organizations to turn small contributions from many people into significant financial support.

- **Diverse Applications:** A wide range of initiatives, including legal defense funds for protestors, emergency relief for communities affected by natural disasters, and funding for creative projects that raise awareness about social issues, have all benefited from crowdfunding.

- **Success Stories:** The "Standing Rock" campaign against the Dakota Access Pipeline used crowdfunding to raise millions of dollars to support the protestors' efforts. Similarly, the "Bring Back Our Girls" campaign used crowdfunding to sustain its advocacy for the release of kidnapped Nigerian schoolgirls.

- **Impact of Crowdfunding:** Crowdfunding democratizes the funding process, allowing activists to bypass traditional funding sources and gain direct support from the public. This grassroots approach not only provides financial resources but also builds a sense of ownership and participation among supporters.

Challenges and Risks of Digital Protest

While digital activism offers many opportunities, it also presents significant challenges and risks. Activists must navigate issues such as surveillance, misinformation, and digital burnout to ensure that their efforts are effective and sustainable.

Surveillance and Privacy

- **Government and Corporate Surveillance:** Activists operating in the digital realm face the constant threat of surveillance from both governments and corporations. Surveillance tactics can include monitoring social media activity, intercepting communications, and using facial recognition technology to identify protestors.

- **Protection Strategies:** To mitigate these risks, activists must adopt digital security practices such as using encrypted messaging apps, virtual private networks (VPNs), and secure browsers. Educating activists about digital hygiene and security protocols is essential to protecting their privacy and the integrity of their movements.

Case Study: The Edward Snowden Revelations:

The disclosures by whistleblower Edward Snowden in 2013 sent shockwaves around the world, revealing the vast and pervasive nature of global surveillance conducted by intelligence agencies, particularly the National Security Agency (NSA) in the United States. Snowden, a former NSA contractor, exposed a range of clandestine programs that were capable of monitoring and collecting data on the communications of millions of people globally, including activists, journalists, and ordinary citizens. These programs not only involved the interception of phone calls and emails but also the mass collection of metadata, which could be analyzed to reveal intimate details about individuals' lives, their associations, and their movements.

For activists, Snowden's revelations were a stark reminder of the profound vulnerabilities they face in the digital age. The extent of government surveillance underscored the ease with which state actors seeking to suppress dissent could intercept their communications, track their movements, and infiltrate their networks. These capabilities, which could identify, target, and neutralize activists and their movements with alarming precision, represented an even more significant threat in countries where repressive regimes already closely monitor and crack down on opposition.

The implications of Snowden's disclosures were far-reaching, prompting a global conversation about privacy, civil liberties, and the ethical limits of state surveillance. For activists, the revelations underscored the urgent need to adopt robust digital security measures to protect themselves and their work from intrusive surveillance. In addition to securing their communications through encryption and using secure messaging platforms, activists also needed to develop a broader understanding of digital hygiene practices to reduce the risks of tracking or monitoring.

Following Snowden's revelations, the activist community began to prioritize digital security in ways that had previously been the domain of only the most tech-savvy. Workshops on encryption, secure browsing, and data protection became commonplace in activist circles, with organizations dedicated to digital rights and privacy, such as the Electronic Frontier Foundation (EFF) and Access Now, leading the charge in educating and equipping activists with the tools they needed to safeguard their operations.

Moreover, Snowden's disclosures spurred a wave of innovation in the development of privacy-focused technologies. From the widespread adoption of end-to-end encryption in popular messaging apps like Signal and WhatsApp to the growth of virtual private networks (VPNs) and secure email services like ProtonMail, the tech landscape began to evolve in response to the demand for greater security and privacy. Activists, journalists, and ordinary citizens alike became more aware of the importance of protecting their digital communications, recognizing that their privacy was not just a personal issue but a critical component of the broader struggle for civil liberties and human rights.

The lessons learned from Snowden's revelations continue to resonate today as the landscape of digital surveillance and repression evolves with advances in technology. Governments around the world continue to develop sophisticated surveillance tools, often under the guise of national security or public safety, that can be deployed to monitor and suppress dissent. For activists, staying ahead of these threats requires ongoing vigilance and adaptation, as well as a commitment to fostering a culture of digital security within their movements.

In summary, Edward Snowden's 2013 disclosures were a watershed moment that exposed the staggering reach of global surveillance and the profound risks it posed to activists and their causes. These revelations galvanized a global movement toward stronger digital security practices, emphasizing the need for activists to protect themselves and their communities from the pervasive eyes of the state. As surveillance technology continues to advance, the lessons from Snowden's disclosures remain crucial in the ongoing fight to preserve privacy, freedom of expression, and the right to organize and dissent in the digital age.

Misinformation and Disinformation

- **The Spread of False Information:** Digital platforms are also vulnerable to the spread of misinformation and disinformation, which can undermine the credibility of movements and sow discord among activists. False information can be used to discredit protests, manipulate public opinion, and create confusion.

- **Combating Misinformation:** Activists must be vigilant in verifying the accuracy of the information they share and in countering false narratives. This can include fact-checking, using reputable sources, and engaging in digital literacy campaigns to educate the public about the dangers of misinformation.

- **Impact on Movements:** Misinformation can have serious consequences for protest movements, leading to a loss of trust and support. By proactively addressing misinformation, activists can protect the integrity of their movements and maintain the confidence of their supporters.

Digital Burnout

- **The Constant Demand of Digital Activism:** The fast-paced nature of digital activism can lead to burnout among activists. The pressure to constantly engage, respond, and produce content can be overwhelming, leading to mental and emotional exhaustion.

- **Strategies for Preventing Burnout:** Activists must prioritize self-care and establish boundaries to prevent burnout. This can include taking regular breaks from social media, delegating tasks, and seeking support from peers and mental health professionals.

- **Sustaining Long-Term Activism:** Sustainable activism requires a balance between digital engagement and offline activities. By pacing themselves and maintaining a healthy work-life balance, activists can remain effective and resilient in the long run.

THE ELECTRIC SLIDE PROTEST

Conclusion

Digital activism has transformed the landscape of protest, offering new tools and strategies for organizing, mobilizing, and effecting change. By harnessing the power of digital platforms, activists can amplify their voices, reach global audiences, and build movements that transcend geographical boundaries. However, these opportunities also present challenges and risks that require careful navigation. As we progress into this new era of activism, we must persistently explore and refine the use of technology to promote social justice, all the while protecting the integrity and welfare of activists. The digital dimension holds limitless possibilities for protest and change, and it is up to us to harness these tools responsibly and effectively in the pursuit of a more just and equitable world.

As we move through the digital landscape, it's important to return to the physical world and the spaces we inhabit. Environmental activism and guerrilla gardening offer powerful examples of how creativity can reshape our surroundings and build sustainable futures. The next chapter explores how green guerrillas are turning urban spaces into battlegrounds for environmental justice and community empowerment.

Toolkit

Checklist for Planning a Digital Activism Campaign:

- Define your goals: Awareness, fundraising, or mobilizing supporters?

- Choose your platforms: Social media, websites, or crowdfunding platforms?

- Create engaging content: Videos, infographics, blogs, or interactive elements?

- Use hashtags: Develop unique and memorable hashtags to unify your campaign.

- Monitor engagement: Track metrics to understand what content resonates most.

Actionable Steps:

- Host a webinar or live stream to discuss the issue with experts and the public.

- Use social media challenges to engage followers and spread the message.

- Develop a resource hub with shareable content for supporters.

CHAPTER 6: GUERILLA GARDENING AND CREATIVE GRASSROOTS PROTESTS

To forget how to dig the earth and to tend the soil is to forget ourselves. –Mahatma Gandhi

Introduction: Cultivating Change
From the Ground Up

Grassroots movements have always been at the forefront of social and environmental change, driven by the power of local communities to take action on issues that matter to them. Whether it's planting gardens in abandoned lots or forming human chains to protest gender discrimination, these movements demonstrate how creativity and collective effort can transform society from the ground up. In this chapter, we explore the intersection of guerrilla gardening and creative grassroots protests, highlighting the unique ways in which communities are using these approaches to address both local and global challenges. Through stories of urban agriculture in Los Angeles and large-scale mobilizations like the Women's Wall in India, we'll see how the seeds of grassroots activism can grow into powerful movements for change.

The Power of Guerrilla Gardening: Reclaiming Urban Spaces

Guerrilla gardening is a form of grassroots activism where people transform neglected urban spaces into green, productive areas. This movement is not just about planting seeds in the earth—it's about planting ideas of self-sufficiency, community empowerment, and resistance to environmental degradation.

- **Ron Finley and the Gangsta Gardeners in Los Angeles:** Ron Finley, known as the "Gangsta Gardener," began his guerrilla gardening journey in South Central Los Angeles, a community plagued by food deserts—areas with little to no access to fresh, healthy food. Frustrated by the lack of nutritious options and the prevalence of fast food, Finley decided to take matters into his own hands. He planted a garden on the parkway in front of his home, transforming a barren strip of land into a lush, productive space. This small act of defiance against the status quo quickly grew into a larger movement.

Finley's vision was simple yet revolutionary: empower residents to grow their own food, reclaim their health, and control their environment. The Gangsta Gardeners, as they became known, turned vacant lots and neglected spaces into vibrant urban gardens, providing fresh produce to communities that would otherwise have limited access. These gardens not only supplied nutritious food but also served as hubs of community engagement, where residents could learn, work, and support each other.

Finley's work has garnered international attention, inspiring countless others to start their own gardening projects and rethink the role of food in their lives. His TED Talk, where he famously stated that "growing your own food is like printing your own money," has become a rallying cry for the guerrilla gardening movement, demonstrating that even small, local actions can lead to significant social change.

Creative Grassroots Protests: From the Garden to the Streets

While guerrilla gardening transforms the physical landscape, creative grassroots protests reshape the social and political landscape. These protests use art, performance, and symbolic actions to challenge the status quo and mobilize communities around issues of justice and equality.

- **The Women's Wall (India, 2019):** One of the most powerful examples of creative grassroots protest is the Women's Wall in Kerala, India. On January 1, 2019, over five million women formed a human wall that stretched over 600 kilometers across the state of Kerala in India. The organizers organized this massive demonstration to promote gender equality and protest against gender discrimination, primarily in response to the controversy surrounding the entry of women of menstruating age into the Sabarimala Temple, a Hindu shrine that had long barred them.

The Women's Wall was not just a simple protest—it was a carefully orchestrated act of resistance that combined traditional protest methods with cultural expressions. The human chain symbolizes the unbroken resolve of women across Kerala to stand against gender discrimination. Cultural performances, including traditional dances, songs, and speeches, accompanied the event, celebrating women's rights and highlighting the importance of gender equality.

The Women's Wall's significance extends beyond its immediate impact on gender issues in Kerala. It drew national and international attention, sparking widespread debate on gender equality and the role of religion in modern society. The event also demonstrated the power of peaceful, large-scale mobilizations to empower communities and challenge deeply entrenched social norms.

Cultivating Effective Grassroots Mobilization

Both guerrilla gardening and creative protests like the Women's Wall illustrate the potential of grassroots movements to inspire change. But effective grassroots mobilization requires more than just creativity—it demands strategic planning, community engagement, and a long-term vision for sustainability:

- **Engaging the Community:** Successful grassroots movements start by engaging the local community. Whether you're planting a garden or organizing a protest, it's essential to involve residents in the planning and execution of the project. This not only ensures that the action is relevant to the community but also fosters a sense of ownership and responsibility.

- **Developing a Strategy:** Clear objectives and a well-thought-out strategy are crucial for any grassroots action. Activists should define their goals, identify their target audience, and choose methods that align with both. Whether it's guerrilla gardening to address food insecurity or forming human chains to protest discrimination, the strategy should consider the available resources and potential obstacles.

- **Maintaining Momentum:** Grassroots movements thrive on momentum, which is sustained through continuous community engagement and visible successes. Celebrating small victories, documenting progress, and sharing stories of impact are all ways to keep the movement energized and growing.

Conclusion: Grassroots Movements —From Seeds to Social Change

Guerrilla gardening and creative grassroots protests share a common theme: the power of local action to create global change. These movements demonstrate that by starting small, with a seed or a symbolic act, we can cultivate larger movements that challenge injustice, inspire communities, and ultimately transform society.

As we face growing challenges like environmental degradation, social inequality, and political oppression, the lessons from these grassroots movements are more relevant than ever. They show us that the fight for a better world begins at the local level, with every garden planted and every voice raised. Using creativity and collective action, we can create a sustainable, just, and equitable future.

Toolkit

- **Checklist for Planning a Guerrilla Gardening or Grassroots Protest:**
    - Identify a location or issue: Choose an area or cause that resonates with the community.
    - Develop a strategy: Outline clear objectives and methods for achieving them.
    - Engage the community: Involve local residents in the planning and execution.

- o   Use creative tactics: Consider art, performance, or symbolic actions.

- o Plan for sustainability: Ensure ongoing engagement and evaluation of success.

- **Actionable Steps:**

  - o   Organize a seed bomb workshop to reclaim neglected spaces.

  - o   Partner with local schools or organizations for long-term projects.

  - o Document and share the movement using social media to inspire people to join.

CHAPTER 7: FLASH MOBS FOR CHANGE

Art has to be involved with moral, philosophical, and intellectual conversations. If you call yourself an artist, this is your responsibility. –Ai Weiwei

Introduction: The Impact of Flash Mobs in Activism

Flash mobs, with their spontaneous and often theatrical nature, have emerged as a powerful tool in modern activism. These sudden gatherings, characterized by their element of surprise and creative expression, are more than just public spectacles— they are strategic acts of protest that capture attention, disrupt the ordinary, and convey powerful messages. This chapter delves into how flash mobs effectively raise awareness and drive social change, elucidating the planning, execution, and reception of these spontaneous events by the public and media.

The Power of Surprise: Organizing Flash Mobs and Spontaneous Events for Social Change

Flash mobs leverage the power of surprise to make an impact. These events' sudden, unexpected nature catches people off guard, compelling them to pay attention and engage with the conveyed message. This spontaneity is a strategic approach that disrupts the status quo and underscores the urgency of the issues under protest.

- **Creating Disruption:** Flash mobs are designed to occur in public spaces where they can disrupt the routine flow of life. By breaking into the ordinary with the extraordinary, these events compel onlookers to pay attention, think critically, and engage with the underlying message. The disruption they create is critical for cutting through the noise of everyday life and making the protest's message unavoidable.

- **Engagement through Creativity:** The use of music, dance, and performance in flash mobs makes them inherently engaging. These creative elements draw people in, making the protest more memorable and impactful. The creativity involved in flash mobs allows activists to communicate complex ideas in ways that are accessible, entertaining, and thought-provoking for the general public.

- **Amplifying the Message:** Flash mobs are often filmed and shared on social media, amplifying their reach far beyond the physical location of the event. The viral potential of these events is immense; a well-executed flash mob can spread across the globe within hours, bringing attention to the cause from a vast and diverse audience. This digital dissemination is crucial for spreading the message and creating a ripple effect that can lead to broader support and action.

Planning Considerations: Location, Timing, and Participant Coordination

While flash mobs appear spontaneous, they require careful

planning and coordination to be successful. Key considerations include choosing the right location, timing the event for maximum impact, and ensuring that participants are well-coordinated and understand their roles.

- **Choosing the Right Location:** The success of a flash mob often relies on the setting. Ideal locations are high-traffic areas where the event will be seen by a large number of people. Public squares, shopping malls, and transportation hubs are common choices, as they offer the visibility needed to reach a broad audience. Additionally, selecting a location with symbolic significance can enhance the protest's message, adding layers of meaning and context to the event.

- **Timing for Maximum Impact:** Timing is another crucial factor in planning a flash mob. Schedule the event during peak hours, when the chosen location is most crowded, to maximize the impact. Additionally, aligning the flash mob with significant dates, such as anniversaries of historical events or public holidays, can add to the protest's relevance and emotional resonance.

- **Participant Coordination:** Successful flash mobs rely on the seamless coordination of participants. Organizers often use encrypted messaging apps or private social media groups to communicate with participants, providing them with detailed instructions and coordinating rehearsals. Ensuring that everyone knows their role and understands the sequence of events is critical to executing a smooth and effective flash mob.

- **Contingency Planning:** Given the spontaneous nature of flash mobs, organizers must be prepared for unexpected challenges, such as interference from authorities, adverse weather conditions, or technical difficulties. Organizers can adapt to changing circumstances and reschedule the event if necessary by developing a contingency plan.

Examples of Flash Mobs That Captured Attention

Various social and political movements have effectively used flash mobs, capturing public attention and leaving a lasting impact. This section highlights some notable examples of flash mobs that successfully conveyed their messages and sparked societal change.

Case Study #1: The Occupy Wall Street Flash Mob

- **Overview:** The Occupy Wall Street movement, which began in 2011, aimed to highlight economic inequality and the influence of corporations on government. The movement became known for its creative forms of protest, including flash mobs that symbolized the struggle of the 99% against the wealthiest 1%.

- **The Silent Flash Mob:** One of the most striking flash mobs organized by Occupy Wall Street was a silent protest held in a public space. Participants, dressed in everyday clothing, suddenly froze in place, holding up signs with messages about economic injustice and corporate greed. The silence and stillness of the participants contrasted sharply with the bustling environment, creating a powerful visual metaphor for the silenced voices of the economically disadvantaged.

- **Media Coverage and Impact:** The media extensively covered the silent flash mob, with images and videos of the event rapidly spreading on social media. The protest not only brought attention to the movement's message but also demonstrated the power of non-verbal, creative protest in conveying complex social issues.

- **Key Takeaway:** The Occupy Wall Street flash

mob exemplifies how silence and synchronized action can create a powerful statement, capturing public attention and amplifying the message of a social movement.

Case Study #2: Flash Mobs for Climate Action

- **Overview:** Climate change has been a focal point for many global protests, with activists using flash mobs as a creative way to demand urgent action. These events often involve choreographed performances that convey the urgency and global nature of the climate crisis.

- **Choreographed Dance for Climate Awareness:** In 2019, climate activists organized a series of flash mobs in cities around the world. Participants gathered in public spaces and performed choreographed dance routines set to songs about the environment. The dance was designed to symbolize the interconnectedness of all life on Earth and the collective responsibility to protect the planet.

- **Global Participation and Reach:** The flash mobs were coordinated to occur simultaneously in multiple cities, including New York, London, Sydney, and Tokyo. This global participation emphasized the universal impact of climate change and the need for a coordinated global response. Social media widely shared videos of the performances, further spreading the message and encouraging others to join the movement.

- **Impact and Legacy:** These climate action flash mobs helped to raise awareness about the urgency of addressing climate change and demonstrated the power of coordinated, global action. The events also served to build solidarity among participants and supporters, strengthening the climate movement.

- **Key Takeaway:** Flash mobs for climate action show how

synchronized global events can effectively raise awareness of pressing environmental issues and generate international support for the cause.

Conclusion: The Lasting Impact of Flash Mobs in Activism

Flash mobs and spontaneous protests harness the power of creativity and surprise to make a significant impact on public consciousness. By disrupting the everyday and turning public spaces into stages for social commentary, these events force people to engage with important issues in a way that is both unexpected and memorable. As these case studies demonstrate, flash mobs have the potential to convey powerful messages, capture media attention, and inspire lasting social change.

As activism continues to evolve in response to new challenges and opportunities, the use of flash mobs and other creative forms of protest will likely remain a vital tool for engaging the public and advancing social justice. These events remind us that even brief, unexpected occurrences can have a profound impact, demonstrating that activism can be as much about imagination and innovation as it is about persistence and resilience.

While flash mobs and spontaneous actions create immediate impact, the ultimate goal of many protests is to influence policy and create lasting change. How can we harness creativity to achieve tangible policy outcomes? The upcoming chapter delves into the strategic alignment of innovative protest tactics with policy objectives to bring about tangible, quantifiable change.

Toolkit

Checklist for Organizing a Flash Mob Protest:

- **Plan your message:** What cause are you supporting, and how will the flash mob highlight it?

- **Choose your location:** Public squares, shopping centers, or transport hubs?

- **Select the format:** Dance, freeze mob, silent protest, or something else?

- **Coordinate participants:** Use online tools to communicate with participants and rehearse.

- **Ensure documentation:** Assign someone to film and photograph the event for sharing.

Actionable Steps:

- **Start a social media event** to recruit participants and build excitement.

- **Create simple, easy-to-learn routines** for participants to follow.

- **Use the flash mob to hand out flyers** or direct people to a website for more information.

CHAPTER 8: CREATIVE POLICY-DRIVEN PROTESTS

Never doubt that a small group of thoughtful, committed citizens can change the world; indeed, it's the only thing that ever has. – Margaret Mead, American Cultural Anthropologist

Introduction: The Potential of Creative Protests to Influence Policy

Creative protests are more than just spectacles of public dissent; they are powerful tools for driving social change and influencing policy. When thoughtfully planned and executed, these innovative forms of activism can capture the attention of both the public and policymakers, leading to significant legislative outcomes. This chapter delves into the strategic connection between creative protests and tangible policy goals; the strategies activists employ to engage lawmakers, and practical instances where protests have directly impacted policy decisions.

Connecting Creative Protests to Tangible Policy Goals and Outcomes

To translate the energy and creativity of protests into actual policy changes, activists must connect their actions to clear and achievable goals. A strategic approach is necessary to align the protest's message with specific legislative objectives, channeling the momentum from public demonstrations into meaningful reform.

Strategic Vision

A clear strategic vision is essential for any protest aiming to influence policy. This vision guides the planning and execution of the protest, ensuring that every action taken serves the broader goal of legislative change.

- **Defining Goals:** The first step in creating a strategic vision is to define specific policy objectives. These goals should be concrete and actionable, such as passing a particular piece of legislation, changing a regulatory policy, or influencing budgetary decisions. Clear goals provide a target for the protest and help to focus efforts on achieving measurable outcomes.

- **Targeting Key Stakeholders:** Identifying and understanding the key stakeholders who have the power to enact the desired policy changes is crucial. These stakeholders may include legislators, government agencies, or corporate leaders. Activists must tailor their messages and tactics to effectively reach and influence these decision-makers.

- **Measuring Impact:** Establishing criteria for success is important for evaluating the effectiveness of the protest. This might include metrics such as media coverage, public support, and, ultimately, the passage of legislation or policy changes. By setting clear benchmarks, activists can assess whether their efforts are moving them closer to their policy goals.

Message Crafting

The effective communication of a creative protest's message also determines its success in influencing policy. Crafting a message that resonates with both the public and policymakers is key to building support and driving change.

- **Simplicity and Clarity:** The message of the protest should be straightforward and easy to understand. We should distill complex ideas into clear, concise statements that slogans, visuals, and speeches can easily communicate. Both the public and policymakers are more likely to capture attention and remember a simple, powerful message.

- **Emotional Appeal:** Emotions are powerful motivators for action. By incorporating storytelling and personal narratives into their messaging, activists can create an emotional connection with their audience. This emotional resonance can drive public support and persuade policymakers to take the protest's demands seriously.

- **Cultural Relevance:** Tying the protest's message to culturally relevant symbols, events, or themes can enhance its impact. Activists can make their message more relatable and compelling by leveraging shared values or popular cultural references, thereby increasing the likelihood of a wider audience embracing it.

Strategies for Ensuring that Creative Activism Leads to Engagement With Policymakers and Real Change

While capturing public attention is an important aspect of creative protests, the ultimate goal is to translate that attention into policy change. This requires deliberate strategies for engaging with policymakers and ensuring that the momentum generated by the protest leads to concrete outcomes.

Building Alliances

Alliances and coalitions can significantly amplify the impact of creative protests. By partnering with organizations, influencers, and community groups, activists can build a broad base of support that is more likely to influence policy decisions.

- **Partnering with NGOs:** Non-governmental organizations (NGOs) often have established relationships with policymakers and a deep understanding of the legislative process. By collaborating with NGOs, activists can gain access to these networks and enhance their ability to advocate for policy change.

- **Engaging Influencers:** Influencers, including celebrities and social media personalities, can help to amplify the protest's message and attract attention from both the public and policymakers. Their involvement can bring credibility to the cause and generate additional media coverage.

- **Community Mobilization:** Engaging grassroots organizations and local communities is essential for demonstrating broad public support for the protest's goals. Community mobilization efforts, such as town hall meetings, local campaigns, and petitions, can show policymakers that the issue has widespread backing, increasing the pressure to act.

Leveraging Media

Media coverage is a crucial tool for amplifying the protest's message and influencing policymakers. The protest can reach a wider audience and effectively communicate its message with a well-executed media strategy.

- **Media Strategies:** It is critical to develop a comprehensive media strategy to maximize the impact of a creative protest. This strategy should include press releases, media kits, and coordinated social media campaigns to ensure consistent messaging across platforms.

- **Visual Impact:** Creative protests often rely on visually striking elements, such as art installations, performances, and symbolic actions, to capture media attention. The media and social media are likely to share these powerful images, thereby extending the protest's reach.

- **Narrative Control:** Controlling the narrative surrounding the protest is vital for ensuring that its message is accurately represented. Activists should be prepared to engage with the media, providing clear explanations of their goals and countering any misinformation or negative portrayals.

Policy Advocacy

Combining creative protests with traditional advocacy techniques can enhance their effectiveness in achieving policy change. Direct engagement with policymakers, along with well-crafted policy proposals, can turn the energy of the protest into tangible legislative outcomes.

- **Direct Lobbying:** Engaging in direct lobbying efforts, such as meetings with legislators, letter-writing campaigns, and testifying at hearings, can complement the impact of creative protests. By presenting policymakers with clear, well-reasoned arguments and evidence, activists can make a compelling case for legislative change.

- **Policy Proposals:** Developing specific policy proposals that provide concrete solutions to the issues highlighted by the protest is essential. These proposals should be based on thorough research and be feasible for implementation, offering a clear path forward for policymakers.

- **Public Hearings and Forums:** Participating in public hearings, forums, and town halls provides an opportunity for activists to directly present their case to policymakers and the public. These platforms allow activists to engage in dialogue, answer questions, and build support for their policy goals.

Where Protests Made Policies

Creative protests have led to significant policy changes throughout history. By examining real-world examples, we can gain insights into the strategies and tactics that have been most effective in turning public demonstrations into legislative victories.

Case Study #1: The Ice Bucket Challenge

- **Overview:** The Ice Bucket Challenge was a viral social media campaign that began in the summer of 2014 to raise awareness and funds for amyotrophic lateral sclerosis (ALS) research. Participants filmed themselves dumping a bucket of ice water over their heads and then challenged others to do the same, all while donating to ALS research.

- **Viral Engagement:** The campaign quickly went viral, with participation from celebrities, athletes, and politicians. This widespread involvement helped to raise awareness of ALS, a disease that was relatively unknown to the general public.

- **Fundraising Impact:** The Ice Bucket Challenge raised over $220 million worldwide, providing a significant boost to ALS research funding. The funds raised were used to support research projects, some of which led to important scientific breakthroughs.

- **Policy Impact:** The increased awareness and funding generated by the campaign also led to greater advocacy for public health policy support for ALS research. Governments and private institutions increased their commitments to funding ALS research, demonstrating the lasting impact of the campaign.

- **Key Takeaway:** The Ice Bucket Challenge shows how a creative and viral campaign can not only raise awareness and funds but also influence public health policy, leading to significant advancements in research and treatment.

Case Study #2: Extinction Rebellion

- **Overview:** Founded in 2018, Extinction Rebellion (XR) is a global environmental movement that employs nonviolent civil disobedience to demand urgent action on climate change. The movement is known for its creative and disruptive tactics, which include road blockades, public art installations, and mass "die-ins."

- **Nonviolent Disruption:** XR's use of nonviolent direct action has been a key element of its strategy. The movement, by disrupting business as usual in major cities, has forced governments and the public to confront the climate crisis and the need for immediate action.

- **Artistic Protests:** XR incorporates art, music, and performance into its protests, creating visually striking and emotionally resonant events. These artistic elements have helped to engage the public and attract media attention, making the movement's message more accessible and impactful.

- **Policy Outcomes:** XR's actions have led to several significant policy outcomes. In the UK, for example, the government declared a climate emergency following XR's protests in London. The movement has also influenced discussions on climate policies in other countries, contributing to a growing global consensus on the need for urgent action.

- **Key Takeaway:** Extinction Rebellion demonstrates the power of combining creative protest with strong policy demands. The movement's use of disruptive tactics and artistic expression has successfully raised awareness of the climate crisis and pushed governments to take action.

Case Study #3: Women of Liberia Mass Action for Peace

Overview: In 2003, amidst the brutal Second Liberian Civil War, a remarkable grassroots movement emerged, led by a group of courageous women in Liberia who were determined to bring an end to the violence that had ravaged their country for years. The movement, known as Women of Liberia Mass Action for Peace, was initiated by social worker and protest organizer Leymah Gbowee. The movement united Christian and Muslim women in a common cause: to demand peace in Liberia. Their relentless efforts played a critical role in pushing for the peace negotiations that ultimately ended the conflict.

Creative Elements: The women of Liberia employed several innovative and nonviolent protest tactics that were deeply rooted in their cultural and social contexts:

- **Sit-ins and Peaceful Demonstrations:** The women organized daily sit-ins and peaceful demonstrations at strategic locations, including outside the Presidential Palace and the Monrovia airfield, where peace talks were taking place. Their physical presence was a powerful symbol of their commitment to peace.

- **Symbolism Through White Clothing:** The women wore simple white T-shirts to symbolize their desire for peace and unity. This visual consistency helped them stand out and conveyed a clear and unified message that was easily recognized.

- **Mass Prayer Vigils:** Recognizing the deep religious faith within their communities, the women held mass prayer vigils, bringing together both Christian and Muslim women to pray for peace. These vigils served as a powerful form of spiritual protest and highlighted the interfaith unity among the women.

- **Sex Strikes:** In a particularly bold and creative move, the women initiated sex strikes, refusing to engage in sexual relations with their husbands until they agreed to support the peace process. This tactic, though controversial, drew significant attention and put additional pressure on male leaders to take the peace negotiations seriously.

Significance: The Women of Liberia Mass Action for Peace is a compelling example of the impact that grassroots, women-led activism can have on national and international policy. Their movement not only contributed to the signing of the Accra Comprehensive Peace Agreement, which ended the Second Liberian Civil War but also paved the way for the election of Liberia's first female president, Ellen Johnson Sirleaf, in 2005.

Leymah Gbowee and the Nobel Peace Prize: Leymah Gbowee's leadership and the Women of Liberia Mass Action for Peace's success did not go unnoticed on the global stage. Gbowee, Ellen Johnson Sirleaf, and Yemeni activist Tawakkol Karman received the Nobel Peace Prize in 2011 for their nonviolent fight for women's safety and their right to full participation in peace-building efforts (Gbowee, 2024). The Nobel Committee recognized Gbowee's extraordinary efforts in mobilizing women across religious and ethnic divides to bring an end to the conflict in Liberia. Her work is a testament to the power of collective action and the crucial role that women can play in peacemaking processes.

Legacy: The legacy of the Women of Liberia Mass Action for Peace extends far beyond the borders of Liberia. It serves as a powerful reminder of the effectiveness of nonviolent protest, particularly when led by women. The movement has inspired similar peace initiatives around the world, demonstrating that even in the face of extreme adversity, ordinary citizens can achieve extraordinary outcomes through creativity, unity, and determination.

Conclusion

Creative policy-driven protests have the potential to influence legislative decisions and achieve major social change. By combining innovative techniques with effective advocacy, activists can produce meaningful results and have a long-term impact on society. The examples and strategies discussed in this chapter illustrate how creativity and strategic planning can turn public demonstrations into powerful tools for policy change, showing that with the right approach, creative protests can do more than capture attention—they can change the world.

Even the most creative and well-intentioned protests face challenges and criticisms. Navigating these obstacles is crucial for sustaining momentum and achieving long-term success. In the next chapter, we delve into the common pitfalls of creative activism, exploring how to overcome them while ensuring that the message remains clear and impactful.

Toolkit

Checklist for Linking Protests to Policy Goals:

- **Define your policy goal:** What specific change do you want to achieve?

- **Identify key stakeholders:** Which policymakers or institutions are you targeting?

- **Develop a message:** Clearly articulate how your protest aligns with your policy goals.

- **Engage with media:** Use press releases, op-eds, and social media to amplify your message.

- **Follow up:** After the protest, continue advocacy efforts through lobbying or public campaigns.

Actionable Steps:

- **Organize a letter-writing campaign** alongside your protest.

- **Set up meetings with local representatives** to present your demands.

- **Create petitions** that directly call for specific policy changes.

CHAPTER 9: CONQUERING THE CHALLENGES & CRITICISMS

First they ignore you. Then they ridicule you. And then they attack you and want to burn you. And then they build monuments to you. –Nicholas Klein

Introduction: The Balancing Act of Creative Protests

Creative protests have the potential to achieve significant social and political impacts, but they also face unique challenges and criticisms. Finding the right balance between creative expression and the serious issue at hand often determines the success of these protests. This chapter explores the complexities of organizing effective creative protests, addressing common criticisms, and learning from less successful attempts to ensure that future actions are impactful and meaningful.

Navigating the Fine Line Between Meaningful Creativity and Minimizing Serious Issues

Creative protests can capture attention and convey powerful messages, but there is always a risk that the creativity may overshadow the seriousness of the issues at hand. Activists must navigate this fine line carefully to ensure that their protests are both impactful and respectful of the causes they champion.

Understanding the Risks

Creative protests, by their very nature, push the boundaries of traditional activism. However, this sometimes has unintended consequences, like trivializing important issues or appearing inappropriate for the context.

- **Tone and Public Perception:** The tone of a protest—whether it is humorous, satirical, or dramatic—can significantly influence how it is perceived by the public. A protest that is too lighthearted might be seen as not taking the issue seriously, while one that is too intense might alienate potential supporters.

- **Cultural Sensitivity:** When planning a creative protest, it is crucial to consider the cultural context and sensitivities of the audience. A bold or innovative action in one culture may be disrespectful or offensive in another.

- **Message Dilution:** There is a risk that the creative elements of a protest might overshadow the core message, leading to confusion or misunderstanding about the protest's goals. If the audience is more focused on the spectacle than the issue, the protest may fail to achieve its intended impact.

Strategies for Maintaining Impact

To ensure that creative protests are effective and respectful, activists can employ several strategies that focus on clear messaging, contextual relevance, and audience engagement.

- **Clear Messaging:** The core message of the protest should be simple, clear, and prominently displayed. All creative elements should support and amplify this message, rather than detract from it. This guarantees that the audience comprehends the issue under discussion and the objectives of the protest.

- **Contextual Relevance:** The creative techniques used in the protest should be appropriate for the context and the issue at hand. This means considering the location, timing, and cultural setting of the protest, as well as the sensitivities of the target audience. By ensuring that the creative approach is relevant to the issue, activists can enhance the impact of their message.

- **Audience Engagement:** Engaging with the audience before, during, and after the protest can help ensure that the message is understood and well-received. This might involve providing context through flyers, social media posts, or speeches, and inviting feedback from participants and observers. By fostering a dialogue, activists can gauge the effectiveness of their protest and make adjustments as needed.

Addressing Criticisms of Creative Protests and Ensuring the Message Doesn't Get Lost in the Medium

Creative protests often face criticism, both from within the activist community and from the public. These criticisms can include accusations of trivializing serious issues, being too disruptive, or failing to produce tangible results. Addressing these criticisms is essential for ensuring that the protest's message remains clear and effective.

- **Trivialization:** Critics may argue that using humor or artistic expression to address serious issues can undermine the gravity of the cause. Activists should counter this by thoughtfully integrating their creative tactics into the protest's overall strategy and communicating the seriousness of the issue in a way that resonates with the audience.

- **Disruption:** Some creative protests, particularly those involving nonviolent direct action or civil disobedience, may be criticized for causing disruption or inconvenience. While disruption can be a powerful tool for drawing attention to an issue, it is important to consider the potential backlash and to plan the protest in a way that maximizes impact while minimizing negative consequences.

- **Effectiveness:** Critics may also question whether creative protests are effective in achieving real change. To counter this, activists must show how their actions align with wider advocacy efforts and contribute to the movement's overall objectives. Providing examples of past successes and articulating a clear strategy for achieving policy change can help to strengthen the credibility of the protest.

Lessons From Less Successful Attempts at Creative Activism

Not all creative protests succeed in achieving their goals. By analyzing examples of less successful creative activism, activists can learn valuable lessons about what works and what doesn't, helping to refine their strategies for future actions.

Case Study Analysis

Examining case studies of creative protests that did not have the desired impact can provide important insights into the potential pitfalls of this approach.

- **Case Study Scenario 1—Misrepresentation Leading to Backlash:** The media and public have often misrepresented or misunderstood creative protests, resulting in backlash instead of support. For instance, the misinterpretation of provocative imagery as offensive or disrespectful could lead to negative media coverage and public outrage in a protest highlighting an issue. Clear messaging and careful consideration of the protest's perception are crucial in this scenario.

- **Case Study Scenario 2—Attention Without Action:** There are also examples of creative protests that successfully captured attention but failed to lead to any meaningful policy change or tangible results. This can happen when a protest generates media buzz but lacks a clear follow-up strategy for engaging policymakers or sustaining momentum. This scenario highlights the need for integrating creative protests with broader advocacy efforts and policy advocacy.

- **Case Study Scenario 3—Insensitivity to Context:** Critics have sometimes criticized creative protests for their perceived insensitivity or inappropriateness towards the issue they aim to tackle. For instance, the use of humor in a protest addressing a sensitive issue such as racial injustice could potentially trivialize the suffering of affected communities. This scenario highlights the significance of cultural sensitivity and the alignment of the creative approach with the severity of the issue.

Learning Lessons From the Past

By analyzing these case studies, activists can identify key lessons that can help them avoid similar pitfalls in the future.

- **The Importance of Context:** Understanding the cultural, social, and political context in which a protest takes place is crucial for ensuring that the message is received as intended. Activists should consider the sensitivities and expectations of their audience and tailor their creative approach accordingly.

- **Clarity of Message:** The core message of the protest must be clear and unmistakable. Creative elements should enhance this message, not obscure it. Activists should regularly check in with their audience to ensure that the message is being understood and that the protest is having the desired impact.

- **Adaptability:** Activists should be prepared to adapt their strategies in response to feedback and criticism. This might involve adjusting the creative approach, refining the message, or finding new ways to engage with the audience. Being open to learning from mistakes and adjusting in real-time can help to ensure the success of the protest.

Conclusion

Creative protests are powerful tools for driving social change, but they are not without their challenges. By carefully navigating the fine line between creativity and respect for the issues at hand, addressing criticism thoughtfully, and learning from past mistakes, activists can maximize the impact of their actions. As we move forward, it is essential to continue refining these strategies to ensure that creative protests remain a force for positive change.

Having explored the challenges of creative activism, it's time to look ahead to the future. What will the next generation of protests look like, and how can activists equip themselves with the tools and knowledge to lead effective movements? The final chapter unveils the secrets of the revolution, offering insights and guidance for the future of protest and activism.

Toolkit

Checklist for Managing Challenges in Creative Activism:

- **Anticipate criticism:** Identify potential areas of criticism and plan your responses.

- **Maintain message clarity:** Ensure that creativity doesn't obscure your core message.

- **Be adaptable:** Prepare to adjust your strategy based on feedback and changing circumstances.

- **Plan for sustainability:** Anticipate the long-term consequences and sustainability of your actions.

- **Build alliances:** Strengthen your movement by collaborating with supportive organizations and individuals.

Actionable Steps:

- **Conduct a SWOT analysis (Strengths, Weaknesses, Opportunities, Threats)** for your campaign.

- **Develop a crisis management plan** for addressing public or media backlash.

- **Hold regular debriefs** with your team to assess progress and refine strategies.

CHAPTER 10: SECRETS OF THE REVOLUTION: THE FUTURE OF PROTESTS FOR THE NEXT GENERATION

Give light, and people will find the way. –Ella Baker

Introduction: The Evolving Landscape of Activism

As the world changes, so too must the strategies and approaches used in the fight for social justice. The future of protests will demand more from activists—more creativity, more resilience, and a deeper understanding of the interconnectedness of global issues. This chapter explores the secrets of the revolution for the next generation, offering insights into the strategies, tools, and mindsets that will empower activists to drive meaningful change.

The Heart of Activism: Leading With Love and Community

THE ELECTRIC SLIDE PROTEST

The intention behind any successful protest is at its core. The future of activism will require protesters to lead from a place of love, care, and community rather than anger, hatred, or resentment. This approach not only builds stronger, more resilient movements but also fosters a culture of inclusivity and mutual respect:

- **Check Your Heart:** Before organizing or participating in a protest, it is crucial to reflect on your motivations. Consider whether your actions stem from a sincere desire to bring about positive change or from feelings of anger and resentment. While anger can be a powerful motivator, it can also lead to actions that are destructive or divisive. Make sure your motivations stem from love and community, concentrating your efforts on enhancing rather than destroying.

- **Protesting with Purpose:** Your goal in protesting should never be to destroy a community or target a specific group out of malice or hate. Instead, aim to create opportunities for dialogue, understanding, and growth. When protests are organized around love, care, and inclusiveness, they are more likely to be embraced by the general public and recognized as a voice of reason. This approach helps to reduce fear, build bridges, and change minds, ultimately leading to more sustainable and impactful outcomes.

- **The High Road of Activism:** This approach focuses on educating individuals, establishing a sense of community, and cultivating an atmosphere that allows for the respectful and empathetic handling of disagreements. Non-violence, open communication, and a commitment to inclusivity are the hallmarks of this approach. By demonstrating a better way of engaging with social issues, activists can create lasting change and inspire others to join their cause. This way, your protest is not just a moment of dissent but a movement toward a better, more just world.

Intersectionality and Inclusivity: A New Paradigm for Protest

The future of protests will be defined by a deeper understanding of intersectionality and inclusivity. Activists will need to recognize the interconnectedness of various social issues and build coalitions that reflect the diversity of the communities they seek to represent.

- **Intersectional Activism:** Future protests will increasingly focus on the intersectionality of issues such as race, gender, class, and environmental justice. Activists will need to address the ways in which these issues overlap and interact, creating more holistic and inclusive movements that resonate with a wider audience.

- **Global Solidarity:** As global challenges like climate change, economic inequality, and human rights violations become more pressing, the future of protests will be marked by increased global solidarity. Activists will need to build alliances across borders, leveraging technology to coordinate actions and share strategies with movements around the world.

- **Inclusivity in Leadership:** The next generation of protests will prioritize inclusive leadership, ensuring that marginalized voices are not only heard but are central to decision-making processes. This shift will require activists to actively challenge existing power structures within movements and to create spaces where diverse perspectives are valued and amplified.

The Digital Revolution: Harnessing

Technology for Activism

Technology has already revolutionized the organization, communication, and execution of protests. In the future, this trend will only accelerate, with new digital tools offering unprecedented opportunities for activism.

The Role of Artificial Intelligence: Enhancing

Activism Through Advanced Technology

As technology continues to evolve, artificial intelligence (AI) is emerging as a powerful tool that can significantly impact the way activists organize, strategize, and protect their movements. AI's ability to process vast amounts of data, automate complex tasks, and adapt to changing circumstances makes it an invaluable resource for modern activism.

- **Automating and Enhancing Social Media Campaigns:** Social media has become a cornerstone of modern activism, providing platforms for spreading messages, organizing events, and rallying supporters. AI has the ability to automate crucial aspects of social media management, freeing activists to concentrate on strategy and guaranteeing the consistent sharing of content across various platforms. AI can also analyze social media trends in real-time, helping activists quickly adapt their strategies to maximize impact.

- **Strategic Planning and Data Analysis:** AI can quickly review a large amount of data and detect patterns and trends more efficiently than human analysis. This capability allows activists to make data-driven decisions, optimize their efforts for maximum impact, and anticipate challenges.

- **Counteracting Surveillance and Censorship:** AI can develop tools to detect and evade surveillance, protect privacy, and ensure secure communication. This is crucial for activists operating in repressive environments where government surveillance is a significant threat.

Virtual and Augmented Reality: Transforming

Activism Through Immersive Experiences

Virtual and augmented reality (VR and AR) are emerging as powerful tools that can revolutionize how activists engage with social issues and mobilize support.

- **Virtual Reality: Creating Global, Immersive Protests:** VR can transport users into fully immersive environments, allowing them to experience events and scenarios as if they were physically present. This opens up possibilities for virtual protests that transcend geographical boundaries, providing a powerful sense of solidarity and collective action.

- **Augmented Reality: Enhancing the Real World with Activist Messages:** AR enhances our interaction with our everyday reality by superimposing digital visual and auditory information onto the real world. Activists can use AR to bring protest messages into public spaces in innovative and attention-grabbing ways, turning everyday environments into dynamic canvases for activism.

- **Engaging Younger Generations and Making Activism More Accessible:** Both VR and AR hold particular appeal for younger generations and can make participation in activism more accessible to those who might otherwise feel disconnected or powerless.

Blockchain and Decentralized Networks

Blockchain technology and decentralized networks offer secure, transparent, and independent means of communication, fundraising, and coordination for activists. These technologies can help future movements resist suppression, maintain integrity, and build resilient networks that are truly by the people and for the people.

Educating for Change: Empowering Through Knowledge

Education will play a central role in the future of protests as activists increasingly recognize the importance of knowledge-sharing and skill-building within movements.

- **Creating Educational Content:** Some of the most effective forms of protest can involve the creation and dissemination of educational content that highlights the history, impact, and significance of the issues at hand.

- **Engaging Your Supporters:** Consistently and accurately conveying the movement's message through workshops, webinars, and study groups reduces the risk of misinformation.

The Legal Landscape: Navigating the Law in Activism

While creativity and innovation are essential components of future protests, it is equally important to navigate the legal landscape with care and understanding.

- **The Importance of Legal Challenges:** Legal activism is a form of protest in its own right—one that requires patience, persistence, and a deep understanding of the law. Future protests will see activists engaging in slow, incremental legal battles that can create lasting change.

- **Understanding Legal Ramifications:** Activists must be prepared for the legal consequences that can arise from their creative protests and be informed about the laws governing protests in their region.

- **Preemptive Legal Support:** Building relationships with legal professionals who support the cause can provide invaluable support before, during, and after protests.

Creativity and Innovation: Reimagining Protest Tactics

As traditional forms of protest become increasingly constrained by legal restrictions and technological surveillance, the future of activism will depend on creativity and innovation.

- **Actionable Art:** Art will continue to be a powerful tool for activism, taking on even more diverse and experimental forms, such as digital graffiti, interactive installations, and virtual reality experiences.

- **Flash Protests and Pop-Up Activism:** The future of protests will see a rise in flash protests and pop-up activism —spontaneous, short-lived actions designed to capture attention and disrupt the ordinary.

- **Hacking and Digital Civil Disobedience:** As activism moves further into the digital realm, hacking, and digital civil disobedience will become more common, requiring thorough research, a strong ethical framework, and legal support.

Resilience and Sustainability: Building Movements that Last

The future of protests will not only be about creating impactful moments but also about building sustainable movements that can endure and grow over time.

- **Mental Health and Wellbeing:** The emotional and psychological toll of activism is significant, and the future of protests will require a greater emphasis on mental health and wellbeing.

- **Long-Term Strategy:** Successful movements will combine short-term actions with long-term strategic planning, ensuring that they can sustain momentum and adapt to changing circumstances.

- **Adaptation and Flexibility:** The ability to adapt and respond to new challenges will be crucial for future protests, enabling movements to remain relevant and effective in a rapidly changing world.

The Power of Collective Action:
Building Stronger Movements

The future of protests will depend on the strength and cohesion of the movements behind them. Activists will need to focus on building solidarity, fostering trust, and creating a sense of shared purpose within their communities.

- **Horizontal Organizing:** Future movements will increasingly adopt horizontal organizing structures where power is distributed more evenly, fostering greater inclusivity and accountability.

- **Building Trust and Solidarity:** Trust and solidarity are the bedrock of any successful movement, and activists will need to invest in building strong relationships within their communities.

- **Celebrating Small Wins:** Recognizing and celebrating small victories along the way can help maintain momentum, boost morale, and reinforce the belief that change is possible.

Conclusion: The Future is Ours to Shape

If we could change ourselves, the tendencies in the world would also change. As a man changes his own nature, so does the attitude of the world change towards him.

I alone cannot change the world, but I can cast a stone across the waters to create many ripples. –Mother Teresa

The future of protests holds immense promise, but it also presents significant challenges. By embracing technology, prioritizing intersectionality, fostering creativity, and building resilience, the next generation of activists can continue to drive meaningful change in the world. The secrets of the revolution lie not just in innovative tactics and bold actions but in the commitment to learning, growing, and adapting as we move forward.

As we look to the future, it's clear that the fight for justice and equality will require a new generation of leaders who are ready to think creatively, act strategically, and stand together in solidarity. The revolution is evolving, and its success depends on future activists learning from and continuing the work of their predecessors. We have the power to shape the future, as well as the responsibility to build a world that is more just, more equitable, and more compassionate for all.

Toolkit

Checklist for Preparing Future Activists:

- **Embrace technology:** Stay informed about emerging digital tools and platforms for activism.

- **Educate and train:** Develop programs to educate the next generation of activists on effective protest strategies.

- **Focus on intersectionality:** Ensure that your movement is inclusive and addresses multiple intersecting issues.

- **Cultivate resilience:** Encourage mental health support and self-care within activist communities.

- **Plan for longevity:** Create structures that ensure your movement can sustain momentum over time.

Actionable Steps:

- **Launch a mentorship program** pairing experienced activists with new participants.

- **Create a digital archive of past protests** to serve as a learning resource.

- **Organize regular strategy sessions** to keep your movement adaptable and forward-thinking.

CONCLUSION: THE TRANSFORMATIVE POWER OF CREATIVE ACTIVISM

If we could change ourselves, the tendencies in the world would also change. As a man changes his own nature, so does the attitude of the world change towards him. –Mohandas Gandhi (1913)

As we draw this journey to a close, it's clear that the power of creative activism lies not just in the imagination but in the courage to take action. The stories, strategies, and insights shared in this book highlight the incredible potential of creativity to disrupt the status quo, inspire change, and build a better future. However, putting these words into action is what will bring them to life.

A Call to Action: Your First Steps

Now is the time to move from inspiration to implementation. Whether you are a seasoned activist or someone new to the cause, there is always a place for your voice and your creativity in the fight for social justice. Here are some actionable steps to take:

- **Join a Protest:** Find a local protest or movement that resonates with you. Show up, stand in solidarity, and lend your voice to the cause. Every person who joins strengthens the movement.

- **Start an Educational Campaign:** If large gatherings aren't your style, consider starting an educational campaign. Use the tools and strategies discussed in this book to create content that informs and inspires others. This could be through social media, a blog, or even a series of workshops.

- **Engage in Legal Challenges:** For those who are drawn to the intricacies of policy and law, your activism might take the form of challenging unjust laws in court. Partner with legal organizations, or support ongoing cases that align with your values.

- **Create Your Own Movement:** Sometimes, the cause you're passionate about isn't being addressed. Don't be afraid to start your own movement. Use the insights from this book as a foundation, and let your creativity guide you.

Encouraging Community: Building Connections

Activism is not a solitary journey; it thrives in the power of community. Connecting with others who share your passion for change can provide support, amplify your message, and increase your impact. Here's how you can start building a community around the ideas in this book:

- **Social Media Engagement:** Join or create social media groups where like-minded individuals can share resources, plan events, and discuss strategies. Use platforms like Facebook, Twitter, or Instagram to build a network of activists.

- **Local Meetups:** Organize or attend local meetups focused on creative activism. This could be a regular gathering at a community center, a local park, or even a coffee shop. These meetups can serve as a space for brainstorming, planning, and connecting with others.

- **Online Forums and Workshops:** Consider creating or joining online forums where activists can exchange ideas, share successes and challenges, and collaborate on projects. You could also organize virtual workshops to help others develop their creative activism skills.

- **Collaborative Projects:** Engage in collaborative projects that allow activists from different areas to work together on a common cause. This could be a global art project, a coordinated social media campaign, or a synchronized day of action.

Sustaining the Movement: A Vision for the Future

The journey of activism is ongoing. It requires perseverance, adaptability, and a continuous infusion of creativity. As you move forward, keep the following in mind:

- **Stay Educated:** The landscape of social justice issues is ever-changing. Stay informed, continue learning, and adapt your strategies to meet new challenges.

- **Support Each Other:** Activism can be demanding, both emotionally and physically. Support your fellow activists, celebrate your victories, and learn from setbacks. A strong community is the backbone of any movement.

- **Think Long-Term:** While it's important to address immediate issues, also consider the long-term impact of your actions. Build movements that are sustainable, inclusive, and capable of growing over time.

Conclusion: A Legacy of Creativity and Change

As you close this book, remember that you are now part of a larger narrative—one that spans generations and continents, and that has shaped the world we live in today. We have passed the torch of creative activism to you, bringing with it the opportunity to illuminate the path for others.

Take the insights, strategies, and inspiration from these pages and turn them into action. Whether it's through art, music, humor, digital campaigns, or direct action, your contributions matter. Together, we can build a future where creativity is not just an expression but a powerful tool for justice and change.

Let this be your call to action. Let this be the beginning of your journey. And let this be the moment you decide to make a difference. The world is waiting for your voice. Go out and make it heard.

Toolkit

Checklist for Sustaining Momentum and Impact:

- **Reflect on achievements:** Regularly evaluate the impact of your activism and celebrate successes.

- **Continue learning:** Stay informed about new tactics, technologies, and social issues.

- **Build a legacy:** Think about how your current activism can inspire future generations.

- **Foster community:** Maintain connections with fellow activists and supporters.

- **Advocate for change:** Keep pushing for the policies and changes you believe in.

Actionable Steps:

- **Develop a resource guide for activists** who want to continue the work you've started.

- **Create a vision statement** for the future of your movement.

- **Host workshops or events** that focus on the continued education and engagement of activists.

CURATED READING LIST FOR THE ELECTRIC SLIDE PROTEST

1. *Beautiful Trouble: A Toolbox for Revolution* **by Andrew Boyd and Dave Oswald Mitchell**

- **Description:** This book is a compendium of stories and tactics from contemporary activists, artists, and political strategists. It offers practical advice and inspiring case studies that align well with the themes of creative protest.

- **Why It's Recommended:** Provides a practical guide to creative activism with real-world examples.

2. *The Art of Protest: Culture and Activism from the Civil Rights Movement to the Streets of Seattle* **by T.V. Reed**

- **Description:** Reed explores how various forms of cultural expression—music, art, performance—have played crucial roles in social movements throughout modern history.

- **Why It's Recommended:** Offers an in-depth look at the intersection of art and activism, which is central to *The Electric Slide Protest*

3. *Rules for Radicals* **by Saul D. Alinsky**

- **Description:** This classic text offers strategies for

community organizing and social change, written by one of the most influential community organizers of the 20th century.

- **Why It's Recommended:** Provides foundational strategies for grassroots activism, which can complement the creative tactics discussed in this book.

4. *This Is an Uprising: How Nonviolent Revolt Is Shaping the Twenty-First Century* by Mark Engler and Paul Engler

- **Description:** The Englers analyze recent movements that have used nonviolent resistance effectively, offering insights into how these tactics can be adapted for future activism.

- **Why It's Recommended:** It provides a contemporary look at successful nonviolent movements, which can inspire readers to think strategically about their protests.

5. *The Revolution Will Not Be Funded: Beyond the Nonprofit Industrial Complex* edited by INCITE! Women of Color Against Violence

- **Description:** This collection critiques the limitations of the nonprofit model and explores alternative ways of organizing and funding activism.

- **Why It's Recommended:** Encourages readers to think critically about how activism is funded and organized, and to explore alternative models that might align with the creative approaches in this book.

6. *How to Change the World: Social Entrepreneurs and the Power of New Ideas* by David Bornstein

- **Description:** This book profiles social entrepreneurs who have developed innovative solutions to some of the world's toughest problems, illustrating how creativity and entrepreneurship can drive social change.

- **Why It's Recommended:** It highlights the role of innovation in social change, aligning with the idea of creative protests.

7. *Direct Action: Protest and the Reinvention of American Radicalism* by L.A. Kauffman

- **Description:** Kauffman traces the history of radical protest in America, offering insights into the strategies that have been most effective in creating change.

- **Why It's Recommended:** It provides a historical context for radical and creative protest tactics, complementing the strategies outlined in this book.

8. *The Activist's Handbook: Winning Social Change in the 21st Century* by Randy Shaw

- **Description:** This handbook offers practical advice on organizing and sustaining social movements, with an emphasis on effective strategies for change.

- **Why It's Recommended:** A practical guide that can serve as a companion to the creative tactics discussed in this book.

9. *The Power of Art* by Simon Schama

- **Description:** This book delves into the history of art and its profound impact on society, exploring how art has been used to inspire and provoke change.

- **Why It's Recommended:** It provides a broader perspective on how art influences society, which can enrich the understanding of protest art discussed in this book.

10. *Creative Community Organizing: A Guide for Rabble-Rousers, Activists, and Quiet Lovers of Justice* by Si Kahn

- **Description:** Kahn offers a guide to organizing that emphasizes the importance of creativity, storytelling, and cultural work in building effective movements.

- **Why It's Recommended:** It aligns closely with the themes of this book, emphasizing the importance of creativity in activism.

ADDITIONAL RECOMMENDATIONS:

- **Podcasts:** *"How to Survive the End of the World"* by Autumn Brown and Adrienne Maree Brown offers discussions on social justice, radical community organizing, and the role of art in activism.

- **Documentaries:** *"13th,"* directed by Ava DuVernay, explores the intersection of race, justice, and mass incarceration in the United States, highlighting the power of documentary film in social change.

- ***Pray the Devil Back to Hell*** by Abigail E. Disney and Gini Reticker chronicles the remarkable story of the Liberian women who came together to end a bloody civil war and bring peace to their shattered country.

- **Websites:** *Beautiful Trouble* (beautifultrouble.org) offers an online toolkit for creative activism, providing additional resources and case studies.

REFERENCES

Ai, W. (2018). *Art has to be involved with moral, philosophical, and intellectual conversations. If you call yourself an artist, this is your responsibility*. Humanity. https://thevividminds.com/quotes/ai-weiwei-on-artists-responsibility/

Antje. (2019, September 5). *Activism and the Power of Humour*. The Commons. https://commonslibrary.org/activism-and-the-power-of-humour/

Baker, E. (n.d.). *Give light, and people will find the way*. Blinkist. https://www.blinkist.com/magazine/posts/empowering-words-ella-baker-quotes?utm_source=cpp

Bell, D. (1996). *Gospel choirs: Psalms of survival for an alien land called home* (1st ed.). BasicBooks. https://www.amazon.com/Gospel-Choirs-Psalms-Survival-Called/dp/0465024130

Brecht, B. (n.d.). *Art is not a mirror held up to reality, but a hammer with which to shape it*. Clotilde Trepy Pastc. https://clotildetrepypastc.wordpress.com/2016/10/06/art-is-not-a-mirror-with-which-to-reflect-reality-but-a-hammer-with-which-to-shape-it-bertolt-brecht/

Burke, S., Berrada, M., & Saenz Cortés, H. (2022). *World Protests: A Study of Key Protest Issues in the 21st Century*. Library. https://library.fes.de/pdf-files/bueros/usa/19020.pdf

Chatham House. (2020, December 15). *What Makes a Successful Protest?* Chathamhouse.org. https://www.chathamhouse.org/2020/12/what-makes-successful-protest

Dylan, B. (1962). *Blowin' in the Wind* [Song]. *Columbia Records. One of Bob Dylan's most famous protest songs, widely associated with the 1960s civil rights and anti-war movements.* Bobdylan. https://www.bobdylan.com/songs/blowin-wind/Watch the song on YouTube

Engler, P. (2022, December 1). *Why movements need to start singing again.* Waging Nonviolence. https://wagingnonviolence.org/2022/12/why-movements-need-revive-song-culture/

Eyerman, R. (2013, June 3). *The Role of the Arts in Political Protest.* Mobilizing Ideas. https://mobilizingideas.wordpress.com/2013/06/03/the-role-of-the-arts-in-political-protest/

Gandhi, M. (1913). If we could change ourselves, the tendencies in the world would also change. *The Collected Works of Mahatma Gandhi* (Vol. XII, April 1913 to December 1914, pp. 156-158). The Publications Division, Ministry of Information and Broadcasting, Government of India. https://quoteinvestigator.com/2017/10/23/be-change/#f+17089+1+2

Gandhi, M. (n.d.). *To forget how to dig the earth and to tend the soil is to forget ourselves.* Peterkalmus. https://peterkalmus.net/books/read-by-chapter-being-the-change/being-the-change-chapter-12-reconnecting-with-mother-earth

Glover, D. (2018). *This is America* [Song]. RCA Records. Performed by Childish Gambino, this song addresses issues of gun violence and systemic racism in America. https://www.youtube.com/watch?v=VYOjWnS4cMY

Goldman, E. (1931). *Living my life.* "If I can't dance to it, it's not my revolution." https://lilith.org/articles/invention-of-a-feminist-sound-bite/

Gunn, R., Aprahamian, S., Park, M., & Bell, S. (2023). Dance and

Protest Special Issue Editorial. https://researchers.mq.edu.au/files/267407070/Publisher_version.pdf

Hart, M. 't. (2007). Humour and Social Protest: An Introduction. *International Review of Social History, 52*, 1–20. https://www.jstor.org/stable/26405479

"I alone cannot change the world..." (2019, June 5). Mother Teresa. https://www.theskippingstone.com/blogs/news/i-alone-cannot-change-the-world-mother-teresa

Kershner, K. (2011, July 25). What is a flash mob? *HowStuffWorks.* https://people.howstuffworks.com/flash-mob.htm

King, M. L., Jr. (n.d.). Our lives begin to end the day we become silent about things that matter. *Unitarian Universalist Association.* https://www.uua.org/worship/words/quote/silent-about-things-matter

Klein, N. (1918). First they ignore you. Then they ridicule you. And then they attack you and want to burn you. And then they build monuments to you. *Amalgamated Clothing Workers of America convention.* Retrieved from [Source]

Marsham, R. (n.d.). Art as Activism: How Protest Art Challenges the Status Quo. *MyArtBroker.* https://www.myartbroker.com/collecting/articles/art-as-activism

Mead, M. (n.d.). Never doubt that a small group of thoughtful, committed citizens can change the world; indeed, it's the only thing that ever has. *BrainyQuote.com.* Retrieved August 31, 2024, from https://www.brainyquote.com/quotes/margaret_mead_100502

Meeropol, A. (1939). *Strange Fruit* [Song]. Commodore Records. Performed by Billie Holiday, this song is a protest against racism and the lynching of African Americans. https://www.npr.org/2012/09/05/158933012/the-strange-story-of-the-man-behind-strange-fruitWatch the song on

YouTube

O'Riordan, D. (1994). *Zombie* [Song]. Island Records. Performed by The Cranberries, this song is a protest against the violence in Northern Ireland. https://www.youtube.com/watch?v=Qj5x6pbJMyU

Ohri, N. (2023, July 31). Youth Engagement in Environmental Activism: Igniting Change for a More Sustainable Future. *World of 8 Billion.* https://www.worldof8billion.org/youth-engagement-in-environmental-activism/

Qualman, E. (n.d.). The power of social media is it forces necessary change. *BrainyQuote.com.* Retrieved August 31, 2024, from https://www.brainyquote.com/quotes/erik_qualman_417503

Ridenhour, C., Sadler, H., Boxley, E., & Drayton, K. (1989). *Fight the Power* [Song]. Def Jam Recordings. Performed by Public Enemy, this song became an anthem for the fight against racial injustice. Retrieved from https://www.youtube.com/watch?v=mmo3HFa2vjg

Srikrishna, R. (2020, August 17). The Power of Protest Art. *Dame Magazine.* https://www.damemagazine.com/2020/08/17/the-power-of-protest-art/

Traditional, & Seeger, P. (1963). *We Shall Overcome* [Song]. Columbia Records. This song, derived from African American spirituals, became the anthem of the Civil Rights Movement in the 1960s. Retrieved from https://en.wikipedia.org/wiki/We_Shall_OvercomeWatch the song on YouTube

Traditional. (n.d.). *Ain't Gonna Let Nobody Turn Me 'Round* [Song]. Popularized during the Civil Rights Movement, with notable versions performed by Joan Baez and the Freedom Singers. https://en.wikipedia.org/wiki/Ain%27t_Gonna_Let_Nobody_Turn_Me_%27RoundWatch the song on YouTube

Traditional. (n.d.). *Bella Ciao* [Song]. Originally an Italian folk song, popularized as an anthem of the anti-fascist resistance during World War II. https://en.wikipedia.org/wiki/Bella_ciao#Watch the song on YouTube

Vidal, G. (1962, January 7). A satirist is a man profoundly revolted by the society in which he lives. His rage takes the form of wit, ridicule, mockery. *The New York Times.* https://archive.nytimes.com/www.nytimes.com/books/97/05/04/reviews/waugh-battle.html?scp=123&sq=end%20of%20the%20world&st=Search#:~:text=By%20GORE%20VIDAL&text=satirist%20is%20a%20man%20profoundly,of%20wit%2C%20ridicule%2C%20mockery.

Watters, R. (n.d.). Digital Activism: The Good, the Bad, the Future. *HAD.* https://had-int.org/digital-activism-the-good-the-bad-the-future/

Wheatley, M. J. (2002). There is no power for change greater than a community discovering what it cares about. In *Turning to one another.* https://en.wikiquote.org/wiki/Margaret_Wheatley

GRATITUDE

Dear Reader,

I sincerely appreciate you purchasing my book and taking the time to delve into its pages. Your support means everything to me, and I am profoundly thankful for the chance to share this journey with you.

As an independent author, your feedback is invaluable in helping my work reach others who might enjoy it. If you found this book captivating or thought provoking, I would be grateful if you could leave a review. Whether brief or detailed, your words amplify the voices of authors like me.

I want you to know that I read every single review. They not only encourage me but also help me grow as a writer. Your thoughts genuinely matter; I'd be delighted to learn how this book connected with you.

Once again, thank you for your support. It means more than words can express. With heartfelt gratitude,

Carrie Love

ABOUT THE AUTHOR

Carrie Love

Carrie Love is a passionate advocate for social change and community empowerment through grassroots organizing, social justice advocacy, and creative protest strategies. With a focus on nonviolent, positive action, Carrie seeks to inspire readers to find their voice and use it to promote meaningful, lasting change in their communities. The Electric Slide Protest is a testament to her belief in the power of unity, creativity, and responsible activism to transform society for the better.

www.ingramcontent.com/pod-product-compliance
Lightning Source LLC
Chambersburg PA
CBHW060504280326
41933CB00014B/2857